Re

100 ESSENTIAL CDs

> THE ROUGH GUIDE

There are more than one hundred and fifty Rough Guide
travel, phrasebook, and music titles, covering destinations
from Amsterdam to Zimbabwe, languages from Czech to
Thai, and musics from World to Opera and Jazz

Other 100 Essential CD titles

Classical Music • Opera • Rock

Rough Guides on the Internet

www.roughguides.com

Rough Guide Credits

Text editors: Greg Ward and Mark Ellingham
Series editor: Mark Ellingham
Typesetting: Helen Ostick

Publishing Information

This first edition published September 1999 by
Rough Guides Ltd, 62–70 Shorts Gardens, London, WC2H 9AB

Distributed by the Penguin Group:
Penguin Books Ltd, 27 Wrights Lane, London W8 5TZ
Penguin Books USA Inc., 375 Hudson Street, New York 10014, USA
Penguin Books Australia Ltd, 487 Maroondah Highway,
PO Box 257, Ringwood, Victoria 3134, Australia
Penguin Books Canada Ltd, 10 Alcorn Avenue,
Toronto, Ontario, Canada M4V 1E4
Penguin Books (NZ) Ltd, 182–190 Wairau Road,
Auckland 10, New Zealand

Typeset in Bembo and Helvetica to an original design by Henry Iles.
Printed in Spain by Graphy Cems.

A catalogue record for this book is available from the British Library.
ISBN 1-85828- 567-4

Reggae

100 ESSENTIAL CDs

THE ROUGH GUIDE

by
Steve Barrow
and
Peter Dalton

Contents List

Introduction

The Rough Guide to Essential Reggae CDs is in some ways a micro-history of the music, a book that ranges from ska and rocksteady to ragga and digital rhythms through celebrating 100 of the best all-time albums. In our selections, we've followed other books in this series by picking (on the whole) just one CD for each artist, though we've had to break the rules for a few key figures – Duke Reid, The Skatalites, Lee Perry, Delroy Wilson, Yabby You – whose careers and albums take in several phases of the music. And reggae being what it is – a singles-driven and producer-driven market – we've opted for a good number of compilations.

Reggae aficionados might be surprised to see a few crucial names missing from our lists. A number of these will be down to taste, but there are some great artists and producers, sadly, who just don't have decent available recordings on CD. Justin Hinds is one such figure: his beautiful Treasure Isle recordings are unavailable at the time of writing because of a legal issue over publishing. Prince Buster currently has nothing from his vast catalogue available, except the excellent (but difficult to find) Japanese issue, *King of Ska*. We made an exception by including this. In general we have tried to select CDs that, in theory at least, are available in chain store reggae sections worldwide. Certainly they will be readily available at competitive prices through specialists like *VP*, *Dub Vendor*, *Greensleeves Mail Order*, or *Ernie*, as well as through many outlets on the Internet.

All the CDs selected in this book are, to the best of our knowledge, legally produced discs on bonafide labels. As will be seen, the Heartbeat label has over a quarter of the selections, principally due to their stewardship of the important Studio One catalogue; elsewhere, independents continue to lead in the re-issue and contemporary fields. The choices of CDs on the Blood & Fire label – associated with co-author Steve Barrow – was made by Peter Dalton, to avoid partiality; though for the record Steve did put his case for the Congos.

As fans of Jamaican music for the last thirty years, we found selecting just 100 essential reggae albums, to reflect this crucial and innovative music in all its phases, a real challenge. We hope that you enjoy our efforts, even if you don't always agree, and that this book will expand the collections and musical enjoyment of newcomers and long-time aficionados alike.

Acknowledgements

We'd like to thank our editors Greg Ward and Mark Ellingham at Rough Guides; everyone at Dub Vendor and Metro Down Beat; Paul Coote, David Corio, Bob Brooks, Aad Brakus, Bob Harding, Roger Dalke, Dave Katz, Pete Holdsworth, Ray Hurford, Charlie Morgan, Colin Moore, Max Romeo, Dennis Alcapone, Bunny Lee, Florent Droguet, and David Rodigan; and the ever-helpful staff at Above Rock, Greensleeves, Jamaican Gold, Heartbeat, Island Records (NY), Jetstar, Moodisc Records (FLA), Nighthawk Records, Pressure Sounds, Virgin, and VP. And, of course, our partners, Susan & Marian.

Steve Barrow and Peter Dalton

The Abyssinians

Satta Massagana

Heartbeat, 1993, US

Recorded 1975–82. The Abyssinians: Bernard Collins (vocals), Lynford Manning (vocals), Donald Manning (vocals). Produced by the Abyssinians.

The Abyssinians were the vocal trio responsible for defining the roots variation of close-harmony singing in the late 1960s. Moving the tradition away from its origins in US soul music, they imbued it with a sombre spiritual feel. Their chosen name made it obvious that they drew their inspiration from the Jamaican cult of Rastafari, and their lyrics about a return to an African paradise were appositely supported by minor-chord melodies that looked to the East rather than the West.

The first Abyssinians' single was recorded in 1969 at Studio One. In retrospect, both songs, Satta Massagana and "Jerusalem", can be seen as harbingers of the imminent roots era, but at the time they were very much out of the ordinary, and Coxsone Dodd declined to release them. "Satta Massagana" was essentially a Rastafarian hymn, with its title drawn from the Ethiopian language, Amharic – in which it means "give thanks" – and its dread slow rhythm was far removed from the generally faster reggae tunes then making waves. Its first (very limited) pressing ultimately appeared a couple of years later, on the group's own Clinch label. After it had become a Jamaican hit, Coxsone released a third track that the trio had cut at Studio One – Declaration Of Rights, which had just as serious a 'cultural' message, and a rhythm that was to be 'versioned' almost as much as "Satta" itself.

More cuts of their first hit followed, including one which featured all three members reciting Biblical phrases in Amharic, plus versions by the deejays Big Youth and Dillinger, the saxophonist Tommy McCook, and the guitarist Ernest Ranglin. Further outstanding records were released on Clinch, such as "Let My Day Be Long", "Poor Jason White", "Leggo Beast", "Licking Sticks", and "Prophecy". Although the Abyssinians were not as prolific as many of their contemporaries in recording for producers other than themselves, singles of equal merit were also issued by Lloyd "Matador" Daley (**Y Mas Gan**), Geoffrey Chung ("Tenayistillin Wandimae"), the Federal subsidiary, Rebel ("Reason Time"), and Tommy Cowan ("Love Comes & Goes").

The **Satta Massagana** CD presents the Abyssinians' stunning debut album – released by Klik Records in the UK in 1976 as *Forward On To Zion* – in digital clarity, and adds four extra tracks to complement the original ten: **Reason Time**, **Leggo Beast** (a slightly different mix of "Licking Sticks"), **There Is No End**, and the early '80s tune **Peculiar Number**. While the cuts of the classic singles – "Satta Massagana", "Declaration Of Rights" and "Y Mas Gan" – are, unfortunately, not the originals, these reworkings are consistently worthwhile, and fit in perfectly with other marvellous tracks such as **The Good Lord**, **I & I** and the sublime **African Race**.

Though Bernard Collins is usually considered the dominant presence in the group, both the Manning brothers make exceptional contributions. The only parallel for the ethereal harmonies they provide here is the similar contribution they made as their brother Carlton Manning's 'Shoes'. Each also wrote several of the songs; Lynford's credits include "Y Mas Gan", **Abendigo** and "There Is No End", while Donald provided "African Race" among others, and co-wrote "Satta" with Bernard Collins. Jamaican harmonies have never reached a higher level – either literally or metaphorically – than on this unforgettable set, and only the *Carlton & His Shoes* debut album for Studio One comes even close to equalling its achievement.

➲ We almost chose **Satta Dub**, Tabou 1, France, 1998

Dennis Alcapone

Forever Version

Heartbeat, 1991, US/UK

Recorded 1971–72. Dennis Alcapone (deejay). Produced by Coxsone Dodd.

Dennis Alcapone was one of the most successful deejays to follow in the immediate wake of U-Roy at the start of the 1970s. As his rapping or toasting style was a more musical version of U-Roy's jive, he styled himself the first "sing-jay". Like U-Roy, he started his career recording sides for producers Keith Hudson and Duke Reid, but it was at Studio One that Alcapone truly perfected his style. There he was lucky enough to link up with studio engineer Sylvan Morris and assistant Larry Marshall, two relatively unsung but highly creative technicians who rose to the challenge of capturing his style on wax.

Alcapone started working with a small sound system called El Paso Hi-Fi in 1968. By the end of 1969, the sound was a well-established favourite among the dance patrons of Kingston's ghettos. El Paso Hi-Fi acquired a loyal following in certain 'bad man' circles; it was a particular favourite of the notorious Jack Massop, the father of Claude Massop, who became a leading enforcer for the conservative JLP (Jamaica Labour Party) during the mid-'70s. Alcapone's debut recordings were also released in 1969; over the next two years he became one of Jamaica's most successful deejays, cutting over two hundred titles. While he enjoyed big radio hits like "Teach The Children" for Duke Reid, and "Guns Don't Argue" for Bunny Lee, the 1971–72 Studio One sessions collected on **Forever Version** capture him at his best, adding his commentary to some of the greatest Studio One hits of the period. Unlike successive generations of deejays, who preferred to ride dub rhythms that featured few or no vocal fragments, Alcapone literally answered back to the singer, blending his comments cleverly with the original vocal so that he appeared a part of it. The tunes Dennis chose for his Studio One album are all bonafide dancehall classics, based on the tunes the deejay featured on his sound in the dancehalls of Kingston, and engineer Morris wisely left liberal portions of these original vocals in place on his mixes. Among those included here are Alcapone's responses to hits by Larry Marshall (the proto-reggae **Nanny Version**), the Cables (the plaintive **Baby Why Version**), Carlton & The Shoes (the fragile **Forever Version**), the Heptones (**Baby Version** and **Sweet Talking Version**), and the Wailers (**Dancing Version**). Morris gives Alcapone's voice just the right amount of reverb, reserving his delay effect for the deejay's trademark interjections of "Yeah yeah YEAH!"

Lyrically Alcapone depended heavily on the reservoir of good-time jive phrases established by mic-men like Count Machuki and U-Roy. His originality within this tradition lay in the manner in which he handled it, and the oft-used phrases gained a new currency with his semi-sung delivery. He also frequently incorporated snatches of nursery rhymes into his lyrics, perhaps slyly changing them; thus on his version of Delroy Wilson's **Run Run**, he throws in the couplet "Baa baa black sheep have you any version? Yes sir, yes sir, a studio full . . ."

Alcapone, who was incidentally the first deejay to adopt a "gangster" stage name, made a further dozen titles for Studio One. His superb versions of the Clarendonians' "You Can't Be Happy", Ken Boothe's "Home Home Home", Horace Andy's "Fever", and Burning Spear's "He Prayed" would have fit nicely on this rather short set – the twelve titles on *Forever Version* run 33 minutes. Happily, however, there is still enough of Dennis Alcapone's insouciant jive and witty microphone persona to make the album a defining moment in Jamaican deejay history.

➲ We almost chose **Musical Liquidator**, Jamaican Gold, Holland, 1995

Doctor Alimantado

Best Dressed Chicken in Town

Greensleeves, 1978, UK; K Records, 1987; UK

Recorded 1972–77. Dr Alimantado (deejay). Produced by Dr Alimantado. Engineers include King Tubby, Lee Perry, Gussie Clarke, Pat Kelly, Philip Smart, Maxie.

Doctor Alimantado – born Winston Thompson, Kingston, Jamaica – was one of the most original deejay stylists to emerge from the sound system scene of Kingston during the early '70s. By the second half of the decade, when most of his best self-produced singles appeared on **Best Dressed Chicken In Town**, the first album released on the Greensleeves label, he was being feted by both punk rock luminaries and reggae aficionados in the UK.

Alimantado's progression from his days on Kingston's Lord Tippertone sound involved the usual freelancing for different producers – under names such as Winston Cool and Winston Prince – plus a highly creative period of self-production. There was also the matter of almost losing his life when hit by a bus in 1977, a close encounter that the self-styled "Ital Surgeon" celebrated with both his best-selling single in Jamaica, "Born For A Purpose" – an atypical singing track for Channel One – and the toasting version, "Life All Over", on his own Ital Sounds label.

While Alimantado's earliest tunes for Scratch and Randy's were solid generic efforts, only the sound effects on "Chapter Of My Heart" and "A Little Love Version 3" hinted at the creative outburst that was to be unleashed with the launching of his own label in 1973. One of the first tracks he produced for himself, **Just the Other Day**, showed that he had incorporated elements from the most successful of the Lord Tippertone graduates, Big Youth; just as important was the imaginative production style, which he continued to develop over the next three years.

Deejays' debut sets often catch them at their freshest, usually presenting the hits that have established them beyond the confines of the dancehall. The first album from Alimantado, which covered the period between 1972 and 1977 when he could do no wrong, certainly falls into this category. Amazingly enough, however, none of the singles here was a major Jamaican hit.

Although the Doctor sported dreadlocks – as shown in the eye-catching cover photograph – he seldom relied on orthodox Rastaspeak. Instead, he seemed to be as interested in the sounds of words as in their meanings; witness how **Ride On** blurs the title and the phrase "right on". Even the dread defiance of **I Killed the Barber** involved a play on words: the wild rhythm employed was a cut of John Holt's Treasure Isle classic "Ali Baba". Manipulating sound was obviously an interest Alimantado shared with Scratch, who engineered four of the tracks here. Their quintessential collaboration, **Best Dressed Chicken In Town** itself, successfully explored the outer limits of both the Black Ark mixing board and the deejay's vocal and lyrical prowess. Half-sung, half-toasted, and built on the rhythm of Horace Andy's "Ain't No Sunshine", it remains one of the most gloriously eccentric Jamaican records ever released. (The aural experiments on the top side of the 45 were taken to their logically insane conclusion on the version, "She Wreng Up".)

A crucial reason why Alimantado's self-productions worked so well is that he was able to persuade producers to hand over their strongest rhythms. Thus his self-defence plea **Gimmie Mi Gun** is delivered over one of Gregory's top sufferer's tunes, "Thief A Man", while the same singer's equally strong "My Religion" supports **Unitone Skank**, and the deejay's commentary on **Poison Flour** is over Horace Andy's "A Quiet Place". But you only have to pick any track to be impressed by the mixture of ingenuity and conviction . . .

➲ We almost chose **Born For A Purpose**, Greensleeves, UK, 1997

Bob Andy

Songbook

Studio One, 1997, US

Recorded 1966–68. Bob Andy (vocals). Musicians include Jackie Mittoo (organ),
Roland Alphonso (sax). Produced by C. S. Dodd.

In comparison to many of his Jamaican contemporaries, Bob Andy – born Keith Anderson, 1944 – has not exactly been prolific. Since starting out in 1964 as a founder member of The Paragons, he has made only nine albums. Three of those feature him alongside Marcia Griffiths as half of the duo Bob & Marcia, who had two big pop-reggae hits in 1970 and 1971. Both "Young Gifted & Black" and "Pied Piper" were recorded for producer/studio owner Harry Johnson, and entered the UK top twenty. Of the remaining six solo albums, the three he released between 1968 and 1978 – **Songbook**, *The Music Inside Me*, and *Lots Of Love & I* – are all characterized by their finely crafted songs, with socially aware lyrics delivered in a soulful vocal style.

Coxsone originally released *Songbook* in the early 1970s. Although all the songs – with the exception of **Life Could Be A Symphony** – had been recorded between 1966 and 1968, and had previously appeared as 45s, they make a remarkably coherent album. Nine of the twelve songs are now regarded as classics, thanks not only to the performances here but also to the number of cover versions they have inspired in the last thirty years. Even bluesman Taj Mahal did a powerful version of "Desperate Lover" (with members of the Wailers) on his appositely titled *Mo' Roots* album in 1974.

Songbook contains six love songs; the remaining selections deal with themes of social and personal growth. They reveal Bob Andy as not only one of the best songwriters working in Jamaica from the mid-1960s, but also an expressive and mature vocalist. His warm style, although occasionally showing the influence of Alton Ellis or Ken Boothe, fits the material perfectly. Vocal harmony on three of the tracks here is provided by Bunny Wailer and Peter Tosh – in fact when Bob Andy first heard himself on **I've Got To Go Back Home**, at a Coxsone dance, even he was tricked into thinking it was the Wailers! Complemented by a beautiful horn arrangement by Coxsone's studio band, the Soul Vendors, the song is a bonafide masterpiece, its theme of being prevented by circumstance from returning home being imparted in terms that are completely individual and at the same time universal. **Crime Don't Pay** features the same lineup, and is directly and forcefully directed to the rudies.

The CD re-release of *Songbook* differs in several respects from the original vinyl release, but none of them really detracts from its impact. Both **Desperate Lover** and **Feeling Soul** are extended versions of the original vinyl issues, embellished with a couple of nice solos. On "Desperate Lover", a tenor-sax obbligato, played by former Skatalite Roland Alphonso, has been dubbed in behind Bob's vocal.

Nonetheless, the album remains essentially as conceived – as *Bob Andy's Songbook* – the only non-original here being a cover of the Motown group the Elgins' **Stay In My Lonely Arms**. Andy's superior songwriting makes this a masterpiece that belongs in anyone's CD collection – and not just of reggae music. This is classic indeed.

Selections from Bob Andy's 1975 album *The Music Inside Me* are available on the *Retrospective* CD mentioned as our alternative below; there are also sleevenotes by the celebrated Jamaican poet Edward Braithwaite, from the original vinyl issue.

➲ We almost chose **Retrospective**, I-ANKA, UK, 1995

Horace Andy

In the Light/In the Light Dub

Hungry Town, 1977, US; Blood & Fire, 1995, UK

Recorded c. 1977. Horace Andy (vcls, gtr), musicians include Augustus Pablo (kbds), Noel Alphonso (drms), Leroy Sibbles (bass), Michael Taylor (bass, kbds), Bobby Kalphat (kbds), Bernard Harvet (kbds), Leroy 'Horsemouth' Wallace (drms). Produced by Horace Andy and Everton DaSilva; dub engineered by Prince Jammy.

When he scored his first hits for Clement Dodd in the early 1970s, Horace Andy – born Horace Hinds in Kingston in 1951 – was responsible for initiating a totally fresh vocal style that has since inspired many imitators. Andy's falsetto, as heard on Studio One classics like "Something On My Mind", "Every Tongue Shall Tell", "See A Man's Face" and the much-versioned "Skylarking", was pitched far higher than even the loftiest tenors of the rock steady era, and evoked feelings of both vulnerability and a transcendental "other worldliness".

Horace Andy's sojourn at Brentford Road proved to be more rewarding artistically than it was financially, and he soon followed the freelance route so common among Jamaican singers. In the first half of the 1970s alone, he notched up hits for producers such as Leonard 'Santic' Chin, Keith Hudson, Derrick Harriott, Harry Johnson, Phil Pratt, Augustus 'Gussie' Clarke and, most notably, Bunny Lee, with whom he enjoyed a particularly enduring musical relationship. In the second half of the decade, and on into the 1980s, he maintained a high profile in the recording studios of Kingston, with additional sessions in New York and London. As well as producing some records for himself, he cut further striking sides for Bunny Lee, and also Augustus Pablo, Joe

Gibbs, Winston Holness, Tappa Zukie, Prince Jazzbo, and Lloyd 'Bullwackie' Barnes. Covering gentle, often pain-wracked love songs and 'cultural' material alike, he built up a formidable reputation among the reggae cognoscenti. By the time the '90s came along, it might have seemed unlikely that this most distinctive of reggae singers would much broaden his audience, but he then enjoyed the greatest popular success of his career, recording two best-selling albums with the Bristol-based UK dance act Massive Attack.

Though many of Andy's finest moments are lost on scarce Jamaican 45s, most of his Studio One work is still available on two seminal sets, *Skylarking* and *The Best Of Horace Andy*, while his strongest album of the late '70s, the phenomenal **In the Light**, has now been made available on CD. Originally released on DaSilva's New York-based Hungry Town label, in 1977, this was a rarity before being coupled with its equally collectible dub counterpart. Even before the vocal album appeared, Andy had made an impression on Hungry Town with two powerful singles, "Youths Of Today" and a recut of the Studio One favourite "New Broom". But what made the album special was the manner in which it stood as a cohesive whole – rather than the usual collection of singles. Andy obviously meant this to be his definitive statement, both looking back to past glories and expressing his current state of mind.

Even a recut of the Studio One hit **Fever** stands comparison with his original, while **In The Light** itself, **Problems**, and **Government Land** are simply awesome. Future ragga producer Lloyd 'Prince Jammy' James sits at the controls for the dub versions. His reconstruction of the vocal set confirms the heavyweight nature of the rhythms, and brings out some even "dreader" textures. Never quite a dub innovator to match his mentor King Tubby, Jammy nevertheless brought something fresh to the mixing board at the tiny studio at 18 Dromilly Avenue; and these versions of the Horace Andy set, alongside the subsequent *In Lion Dub Style* album, represent his peak as a dub engineer.

⮑ **We almost chose Skylarking**, Studio One, US

Anthony B

Real Revolutionary

Greensleeves, 1996, UK

Recorded early 1990s. Musicians include Sly & Robbie, Mafia & Fluxy, Firehouse Crew, Jazwad, Earl Chinna Smith, Cat Coore and Dean Fraser. Produced by Richard Bell.

Anthony B (born Keith Anthony Blair, Clarks Town, Jamaica) is in the vanguard of the new roots revival that has become a major trend of 1990s Jamaican music. **Real Revolutionary** (also released as *So Many Things*) was the album that put him there – and deservedly so. This is as radical an album as anyone in Jamaica has produced in the '90s.

Anthony B comes from a religious family - his grandmother was active in the Revivalist church, his mother a Seventh Day Adventist – and as a youth he attended church on Saturday and Sunday, developing his vocal skills in the Trelawny choirs, before debuting on his local sound system, Shaggy Hi-Power. He moved to Portmore in 1988, dejaying on a set called Lovers Choice that also featured Mega Banton and Ricky General. When they recorded for the Wizard label owned by E. Parara in 1993, Anthony B got the chance to record his debut single, a duet called "Living Is Hard", made with his friend Little Devon (Devon Morgan).

Devon introduced Anthony to Richard Bell, owner of the Star Trail label, and he immediately began recording for him, issuing early singles like "Don't Red Eye" and **Repentance Time**, which drew attention. However, when Anthony chanted **Fire Pon Rome** on the Boxing Day 'Sting' in December 1995 it caused a sensation. The lyric was a scathing attack on the

Jamaican establishment, with Anthony naming names and blasting the policies and politics of all the major parties – PNP Prime Minister P.J. Patterson, former JLP PM Edward Seaga, and Bruce Golding's National Democratic Movement. The Pope is also 'burned' lyrically, in Bobo Dread style: the Vatican is seen by Rastas as responsible for financing and blessing the slave trade. The record was banned from airplay, not only in Jamaica, but elsewhere in the Caribbean and even on Miami radio reggae shows. Anthony's next single, Swarm Me, answered the critics, claiming rights of free speech and concluding defiantly: "Now we a fling fire under dem heel / Ask dem why they want all the truth conceal / That's why dem come swarm me / Say me start a revolution army / You nah see dem lose? / This is the generation dem can't confuse." Other hits, including Rumour and the excellent Raid Di Barn, soon followed.

Gathered together on the Real Revolutionary set, released in 1996, the songs met major critical acclaim with reviewers noting the similarity in attitude to the late Peter Tosh. The disc was a showcase for Anthony's incisive and thoughtful lyrics, collecting early singles for Star Trail along with previously unreleased songs. Most are delivered in a chanted, half-sung style. Particularly effective is his version of Tracy Chapman's Cold Feet, a tale of a youth who gets involved in guns and pays the price; Anthony makes it sound like he wrote it. Indeed, the whole set bears the stamp of a genuine and original talent.

Real Revolutionary's success meant that producers who had previously recorded Anthony B rushed singles onto the market; by mid-1999, well over a hundred had been issued on a variety of labels. Unlike many artists, Anthony has professional management and tours Europe and the US; he made a big impression at the London Essential Music Festival in August 1998, stealing the show from such as Cocoa Tea and U-Roy. His second album Universal Struggle was also released that year, while Star Trail issued a set featuring him alongside the similarly uncompromising and Bobo-influenced Sizzla.

⮕ We almost chose **Universal Struggle**, VP, US, 1998

Aswad

Roots Rocking: The Island Anthology

Island Jamaica, 1997, US

Recorded 1976–90. Aswad: Brinsley 'Dan' Forde (gtr, vcls), Tony 'Gad' Robinson (vcals, kbds, bass), Angus 'Drummie Zeb' Gaye (drms), George Oban (bass), Martin 'Tata' Augustine (gtr). Producers include Michael Campbell, Aswad, Gussie Clarke.

Aswad, who take their name from the Amharic word for 'black', have been a much-esteemed fixture on the British reggae scene since the mid-1970s. Popular from the beginning with the roots fraternity in the UK, they achieved real commercial success in the 1980s, first with "Chasing the Breeze" (not included here) and then the chart-topping – and just as delightful – **Don't Turn Around**.

Aswad have always been a self-contained band, providing their own rhythms in addition to some of the finest reggae vocals recorded in Britain. When they formed in 1975, in the Westbourne Grove area of West London, their nucleus was Brinsley 'Dan' Forde, George Oban, Tony 'Gad' Robinson, and Angus 'Drummie Zeb' Gaye. After Oban left in 1980, Robinson took on his bass duties. Additional players have drifted in and out of the outfit for both studio and live work, including the vintage Jamaican trombonist Vin 'Don D Junior' Gordon, the trumpeter Eddie 'Tan Tan' Thornton, and Michael 'Bammi' Rose (all of whom contributed to the classic militant steppers instrumental of 1979, **Warrior Charge**).

Although Aswad's forays into pop territory – "Don't Turn Around" in 1988 was followed by **On And On** the next year – lost them part of their original following, the *Nineties Too Wicked* album, recorded at Gussie Clarke's Music Works studio in Kingston, showed they could return to their roots whenever they felt like it. The track with ragga DJ Shabba Ranks, **Fire**, particularly stood out from this session for being as dancehall rough as anything from their acclaimed live album from the 1983 Notting Hill Carnival.

The only things that the superbly packaged two-disc, 34-track **Roots Rocking** anthology misses from Aswad's long and varied career are any cuts from their classic 1981 album for CBS, *New Chapter*, or its follow-up *Not Satisfied*. Nevertheless, brilliant live renditions of two tracks from the former, **Tuff We Tuff** and **African Children**, plus **Not Satisfied** and **Drum & Bass Line** from the latter, cover that period in fine style. So too, in a different way, does the dub of the ultra-heavy "Love Fire", taken from the excellent *A New Chapter Of Dub* (which, though the dub counterpart to their CBS debut set, appeared on Island).

Listening to tracks recorded over a fourteen-year period, from 1976 to 1990, one's overwhelming impression is of the excellent musicianship and sense of taste which Aswad brought to almost every facet of reggae – as the music, as well as the band themselves, developed through two decades. Perhaps their greatest strength lay in their refusal ever to restrict themselves to one style alone; instead, Aswad continually moved forward. Thus their story begins with roots rocking from 1976 which was clearly inspired by the Island-signed Wailers, leads through more militant steppers tracks from the end of the 1970s, then on to the band's dancehall and lovers-rock phases of the early 1980s, and on further to poppier material. Despite a mass of musical styles and rhythms, a clear identity as Aswad is always maintained. The pop-reggae values of a track like **Smile** connect just as surely as "Warrior Charge", the rootsiest anthem on offer. And the band are just as assured touching on all of the points in between. All the evidence needed that Aswad are the greatest reggae band in the studio outside of Jamaica, and possibly the ultimate in live appearances anywhere.

⮑ We almost chose **Showcase**, Island, UK 1980

Buju Banton

'Til Shiloh

Loose Cannon, 1995, UK

Recorded 1995. Buju Banton (deejay). Producers include Donovan Germain, Buju Banton, Steely and Clevie, Dave Kelly, Bobby Digital and Sylvester Gordon.

Until the early '90s, ragga, the hard-edged music that has reigned in Jamaican dancehalls since 1985, was almost universally associated with guntalk and slack (sexually explicit) lyrics. Then, as a new generation of 'conscious' singers came to the fore, several deejays who had made their names with hardcore images and themes joined vocalists like Garnett Silk in chanting down the iniquities of Babylon or praising a more righteous way of life. The senseless shooting of the promising young chatter Panhead, in 1993, was a major factor in the process. Buju Banton – born Mark Myrie in Kingston in 1973 – seemed particularly affected by the death of his friend. In 1992 he had achieved considerable notoriety among liberal commentators (who don't usually pay much heed to the utterances of Jamaican deejays) with the homophobic "Boom Bye Bye". The following year, he came up with the hard-hitting **Murderer**, a tune that was instrumental in changing the focus of deejay lyrics away from celebrations of the gun.

The youthful Buju had also started growing dreadlocks and listening to the deliberations of Rasta elders, though clearly he still had no problems in rocking the dance with Jamaican hits like the celebratory **Champion**. Another best-seller in 1994, one expressing a new maturity and thoughtfulness, was "Operation Willy", a safe sex number from which all proceeds were donated to a Kingston home for children with AIDS. At the end of the same year, he was able to launch the first of his own labels, CB 321, with the singularly uncompromising Rampage, featuring a strong anti-gun message over a hardcore dancehall rhythm. Further expressions of Rasta-consciousness came in 1994, with "God of My Salvation", and the next year with the angry "Sensimelia Persecution", and an updating of Marcia Griffiths' classic "Stepping Out Of Babylon" (retitled "Stepping To Mount Zion", and featuring the former I-Three herself, along-side Buju's fellow deejays Cobra, Tony Rebel and Beenie Man).

Even the impact of these singles didn't quite prepare the world for the brilliantly conceived 'Til Shiloh set, Buju's third for producer Donovan Germain, which was also released in 1995. Centering on the productions of Germain, it would rank as essential just for two of its most reflective, cultural tracks: 'Til I'm Laid To Rest and the wondrous Untold Stories. The latter, a semi-accoustic number that brings to mind Marley's "Redemption Song", includes such biting couplets as: "All I see is people ripping and robbing and grabbing / No love for the people who are sure suffering real bad / Another toll to the poll may God help we soul / What is to stop the youth getting out of control / Filled up with education and yet don't own a payroll / The clothes on my back has countless eye holes."

As it is, nothing else falls far short of their exalted standard. The former Penthouse single "Murderer" and a version of Garnett Silk's Complaint continue the 'conscious' feel of an album that was clearly the product of much time and thought. Demonstrating Banton still to be very much in touch with his dancehall followers, some tracks are as raggamuffin-rough as any-thing he had previously voiced – including Only Man, Chuck It So, and What Ya Gonna Do? (with the sweet-voiced dancehall favourite Wayne Wonder).

Certainly an album to be heard by anyone who still thinks of ragga as somehow a betrayal of reggae's past glories.

⮑ We almost chose **Voice of Jamaica**, Mercury, US, 1993

Starky Banton

Powers Youth

Fashion, 1997, UK

Recorded 1997. Starky Banton (deejay). Produced by Dub Organiser.

Not only among Jamaican performers, but also in the UK, reggae in the '90s saw a turning away from guntalk and slackness, and a return to 'cultural' themes. While the young Sizzla, along with the more established Buju Banton and Capleton, led the way for 'cultural' deejays in Kingston, among the figures in London who picked up on this salutary influence were both Chukki Starr and Starky Banton. Recording respectively for Neil 'Mad Professor' Fraser and the Fashion set-up, both have made superb albums, but **Powers Youth** has the slight edge, largely because each of the deejay's tracks is followed by a blistering dub version.

Born David Murray in London in 1962, Starky Banton first came to public attention with his amusingly dismissive thoughts on the 'jungle' phenomenon – "One bag a noise and a whole heap a sample / That's something my ear holes can't handle!" After "Jungle Bungle" (not included here) had made its impression on the UK reggae chart, Banton turned his attention to the sort of topics he obviously thought were the most fitting for his own music – what in the 1970s had been called 'truth and rights.' After a version of Mykal Rose's recut of I Love King Selassie in 1996, which employed a sample from Bob Marley's "Natural Mystic", there followed a couple of superb 10-inch singles the following year. Released on a newly designed label from Fashion, styled on King Tubby's legendary dubplates imprint, they impressed both with their vintage-style dubs and with the deejay's militant pronouncements. **I & I Saw Them Coming**, which appeared first, featured a late-1970s style bass line, as well as an equally vintage declaration of Banton's Rastafarian beliefs: "I & I saw dem coming / But I know I won't be running / No, no, no, I stand on solid ground." The sentiments were made all the more convincing by the deejay's assured half-spoken, half-chanting delivery. The three further versions contained on the 10-inch included a melodica cut, while the mixes – credited to the Dub Organiser – were far more subtle than most recent UK attempts in this direction, and fully brought out the qualities of the exceptionally strong rhythm. Both sides of the follow-up, "Weeping & Wailing"/"Rastaman Chant", were every bit as powerful and credible.

A debut album, *Powers Youth*, arrived later in 1997, building on the success of the singles. Everyone present at the sessions at the A-Class Studio was impressed by Banton's fervour, and the way he very obviously meant every word he chanted so right-eously into the mike; thankfully, these are just the qualities that were captured in the recordings. On the opening track, **Nah Badda Tell Me**, he proclaims his message to Mr Babylon that he shouldn't bother to trick him with his ideology, "nah brain-wash me with your false history / For I & I nah bow to your monarchy / Rastaman, I a praise his majesty." While neither side of his second 10-inch is included, the thunderous "I & I Saw Dem Coming" is here in all its glory, as is his inspired version of "I Love King Selassie". All the other tracks were making their first appearance, but more than lived up to expectations.

The real horns on *Powers Youth*'s heavyweight rhythms bring to mind vintage Channel One, as does the inspired mixing (plenty of the 'submarine' noises associated with late-1970s' Maxfield Avenue productions). Yet for all the backward glances, it's obvious that full use was made of modern studio technology, and the sound couldn't be sharper. Any suspicions about modern UK roots are well and truly nullified by this totally successful set.

➲ We almost chose **Chukki Star/Ghetto Youths**, Ariwa, UK/Ras, US, 1999

Beenie Man

Many Moods Of Moses

Jet Star, 1997, UK

Recorded 1997. Beenie Man (deejay). Producers include Sly & Robbie, Jeremy Harding, Buju Banton, Beenie Man, Handel Tucker, Bob Patin and the Shocking Vibes Crew.

There's a moment on the 1983 soundclash album *King Stur-Gav vs. Lee's Hi-Fi* – recently reissued by Rasslin Records – where deejay Johnny Ringo introduces the nine-year-old Beenie Man, who proceeds to deliver some alarmingly precocious lyrics and tear down the dance. **Many Moods Of Moses** catches the deejay some fifteen years later, at the top of the pile. Amazingly, Beenie Man – born Moses Davis in Kingston in August 1973 – was deejaying at the age of five, on his uncle Sid Knowles' Master Blaster sound system. He recorded his first single ("Too Fancy") for Henry 'Junjo' Lawes in 1982, while deejaying for sounds like Gemini and Lee's. Around this time Beenie and his lifelong friend Little Kirk met up with producer Patrick Roberts, who would play a significant part in their careers. Veteran producer Bunny Lee released Beenie's first album, *The Ten Year Old Wonder*, late in 1983.

By 1987, when Harry J released "In The Spirit" and "Love Have Fi Come", Beenie had appeared on his first big stage shows, DJ Roll Call and Sting '87. Soundman Jack Scorpio issued "Follow Back A We" in 1988, the same year that Patrick Roberts set up Shocking Vibes with Beenie, Kirk and Tonto Metro, releasing "We Run Things", a modest hit, followed by "Kip Wey" in 1989. Beenie also worked with King Jammy at this time, appearing on a couple of discs with fellow deejay Risto Benji. These early efforts were generic deejay tunes, but all the while, Beenie Man was refining his microphone technique.

None of this prepared listeners for what was to come from 1993 onwards. Beenie unleashed a flood of singles, including his first big hit "Wicked Man", and staked his claim as contender for the dancehall crown then held by Buju Banton. In 1994 he finally made it, with two titles in the RJR top five, the huge "World Dance" and "Matie". He and Bounty Killer continued the rivalry they had begun on Sting '93; while Beenie's "Slam" beat Bounty's "Cellular Phone" in 1995's chart, in 1996 Bounty's "Fed Up" pipped Beenie's "Ole Dawg" and "Nuff Gal".

The last couple of years have seen Beenie Man completely eclipse Bounty Killer to become Jamaica's dominant dancehall deejay, as demonstrated conclusively on *Many Moods of Moses*, a Grammy-nominated set from late 1997 that combines then-recent hits with further Shocking Vibes productions. Several tracks feature vocal group A.R.P; they actually introduce the disc with a brief rendition of the South African song "Wimoweh" (aka "The Lion Sleeps Tonight"). There are massive tunes like Oysters and Conch, written with longtime collaborator Anthony Kelly, and Foundation from Sly & Robbie's Taxi label riding a buoyant cut of the "Beardman Ska" rhythm. Who Am I, a UK hit in 1998, sits on a superb hardcore dancehall rhythm called "Playground", built by musician-producer Jeremy Harding. It's a varied programme, with the deejay's renowned versatility manifested through more reflective pieces like Steve Biko; other tracks feature the queen of dancehall, Lady Saw (So Hot) and Buju Banton (Woman A Sample), while Ain't Gonna Figure It Yet has Beenie on a genuine country and western song, actually recorded in Nashville.

At the time of writing, Beenie Man is set to tour Europe with new dancehall sensation Mr Vegas. His determination to stay at the top informs every record he makes; if he continues with the same consistency, it's hard to see who could topple him.

➲ We almost chose **Maestro**, Greensleeves, UK, 1996

Big Youth

Screaming Target

Gussie, 1973, JA; Trojan, 1989, UK

Recorded 1972. Big Youth (deejay). Produced by Augustus 'Gussie' Clarke.

Once U-Roy had kickstarted the deejay phenomenon in 1969, the next major development in this most dynamic of the many facets of reggae was initiated by the top man at the mike from a Kingston sound system called Lord Tippertone Hi-Fi. Born in Jamaica in 1955 as Augustus Buchanan, he went under the name of Big Youth, and was reputedly the first reggae performer to take off his tam and wave his dreadlocks on stage. This defiant proclamation of Rastafarian beliefs – a couple of years before such displays became only too conventional – always caused a sensation. More significant, however, was Big Youth's adaptation of the nature of deejaying. While U-Roy and his immediate followers exhorted dancers to further effort, or responded to the lyrics of the original vocal they were toasting, Big Youth used the form to comment on his own social and spiritual concerns. His delivery was also different: rather than the jivetalk influenced by American radio deejays, he possessed a chant-like style that placed the deejay even more centre stage – and went beyond mere entertainment.

To judge by the sleeve photograph, Big Youth's dreadlocks were just starting to grow when his debut album, **Screaming Target**, was released in 1973. One of the great strengths of this mould-shattering set was that it was produced by a fellow youth-man who was just as eager to prove himself as the young deejay. A childhood friend, Augustus 'Gussie' Clarke was barely twenty himself, and certainly in touch with whatever the current vibe was on the West Kingston streets. Although he had only been producing for about a year, scoring his first hit with U-Roy's "The Higher the Mountain", he already had several suitable rhythms for Big Youth – crisp reggae ones rather than the rock steady favourites that gave U-Roy his early hits – as well as having access to hard-edged tracks from Glen Brown, Tuff Gong, and the African Museum label of Gregory Isaacs and Errol Dunkley. Some of the Big Youth toasts collected here had already been Jamaican hits; the largest was **Screaming Target** itself, one of several recent tunes inspired by violent movies. The rhythm was K.C. White's interpretation of Dawn Penn's Studio One classic, "No, No, No", which had helped establish Gussie's reputation for well-produced, no-nonsense records. Gussie had released two different mixes on single; only one found its way onto the original Jamaican album (the first on Gussie's label), but both are included on this CD re-release, and the flip side, **Concrete Jungle**, which utilized the same rhythm, closes the set. A slightly different cut of **Tippertone Rock**, a tribute to the deejay's sound system, had also appeared as a single, while **The Killer** – alongside the Keith Hudson-produced "Ace Ninety Skank" – had provided many UK listeners' introduction to Big Youth in the summer of 1972.

Exceptional rhythms borrowed by Gussie from other producers included those originally employed for Leroy Smart's "Pride and Ambition" (**Pride & Joy Rock**), Lloyd Parks's "Slaving" (**Honesty**), Dennis Brown's "In Their Own Way" (**Be Careful**) and Gregory Isaacs's "One One Cocoa Fill Basket" (**One Of These Fine Days**) – arguably the strongest records those singers had so far released. How Big Youth developed the style showcased here can be heard on the *Everyday Skank* compilation and *Natty Cultural Dread*, but *Screaming Target* represents him at his freshest. It catches him on the cusp between jivetalk designed to keep dancehalls rocking, and the type of performance that combined the role of a newspaper with that of a prophet.

⮑ We almost chose **The Chanting Dread . . .** , Heartbeat, US, 1983

Black Uhuru

Guess Who's Coming To Dinner

Taxi, 1980, JA; Heartbeat, 1987, US/UK

Recorded 1979–80. Black Uhuru: Michael Rose (vocals), Derrick 'Ducky' Simpson (vocals), Sandra 'Puma' Jones (vocals). Produced by Sly Dunbar and Robbie Shakespeare.

The story of Black Uhuru began in the Waterhouse ghetto of West Kingston, in the early 1970s. The original members of the group – Derrick 'Ducky' Simpson, Garth Dennis and Don McCarlos – cut a version of Curtis Mayfield's "(Romancing To The) Folk Song" for Tommy Cowan's Top Cat label in 1972. It wasn't a hit, and after a couple more tunes the trio broke up. McCarlos went solo as Don Carlos, while Dennis left to join the Wailing Souls in 1976. A youth singer called Michael Rose then joined Ducky and Errol Nelson to form the second version of Black Uhuru. Rose had already cut a few records. including the original version of **Guess Who's Coming To Dinner**, and "Clap The Barber", for Winston 'Niney' Holness. He also made the storming "Running Around" at Channel One in mid-1976, with his friend Winston Campbell. Drummer Sly Dunbar and bassist Robbie Shakespeare played the rhythm, and Rose cut a version of Ken Boothe's "Artibella" for their Taxi label later that year.

Uhuru's debut album, 1977's *Love Crisis*, was one of the first productions of the great engineer/soundman Lloyd 'Prince Jammy' James. With the trademark Uhuru sound evident on tracks like "I Love King Selassie" and "African Love", it sold well in the UK. However, Errol Nelson returned to his former group, the Jayes, and the US-born Sandra 'Puma' Jones, who had come to Jamaica in the mid-'70s to work on a government housing project, took his place. Her plaintive harmony blended well with Ducky Simpson, and provided the perfect foil for Michael's fiery, slur-embellished chants. His singing had now lost its earlier Dennis Brown influences; the new style became known as 'Waterhouse', after the Kingston ghetto that was also home to Don Carlos, Lacksley Castell, and Junior Reid, all of whom sang in a slightly 'flat' vibrato-less style, and used similar vocal tricks and slurs.

It fell to Sly Dunbar and Robbie Shakespeare to provide a musical framework in which the new vocal trio could flourish – usually a quartet of drums, bass, piano or organ (Winston Wright or Keith Sterling) and guitar (Rad 'Duggie' Bryan). After recording "Rent Man" and "Wood For My Fire" for Dennis Brown's DEB label, they consolidated these early successes with covers of the Wailers' "Let Him Go" (for Taxi) and "Sun Is Shining" (Channel One), not yet available on CD.

Black Uhuru's subsequent singles for Taxi were collected on an album that was titled *Showcase* for its original Jamaican release, and later issued on CD as **Guess Who's Coming To Dinner**. The titles here are presented in extended form, with dub section following the vocal, as on the original 12-inch singles. Tunes like General Penitentary, Shine Eye Girl, and Leaving To Zion and Plastic Smile were hugely popular in the dancehall in 1980, and also crossed over to a wider audience when released on Virgin in the UK. The group then moved to Island Records, for whom they recorded four studio albums, including the Grammy-nominated *Anthem*, before they split up. Ducky enlisted Junior Reid to sing lead for a couple of albums, but he returned to his solo career, and the group soon also lost Puma, who died of cancer in January 1990. Ducky has since reformed the original lineup with Don Carlos, once again. Meanwhile, Waterhouse vocal style – as defined by Black Uhuru on this CD – lives on.

➲ We almost chose **Liberation: Island Anthology**, Polygram, US, 1993

Ken Boothe

Mr Rock Steady

Studio One, 1997, US

Recorded 1963–67. Ken Boothe (vocals). Produced by Coxsone Dodd.

Just as ska developed from boogie-based US r'n'b, so rock steady grew from soul; from the mid-'60s, soul-influenced vocalists and groups ruled Jamaican dancehalls. The period when the transition from ska to rock steady took place, between 1965 and 1967, is perfectly captured on **Mr Rock Steady**. Ken Boothe, who was born in Kingston in 1948, came from a musical family; his sister Hyacinth was a vocalist on Vere Johns Jr's talent shows in the '50s. As the '60s dawned, Ken was ready to follow. Vocal duos – either all-male or "boy/girl" – featured strongly in Jamaican r'n'b and early ska, taking their lead from US models like Gene and Eunice, Don and Dewey, or Shirley and Lee. Thus the male partnerships of Bunny and Skully, Alton and Eddie, Higgs and Wilson, and the Blues Busters, as well as mixed duos like Keith and Enid, Derrick and Patsy, and Roy and Millie, all enjoyed success during this era.

Ken's first mentor, Wilburn 'Stranger' Cole, had sung with both Patsy and Millie, as well as scoring big solo hits for Duke Reid. Together they began rehearsing in the ghetto location known as "Back A Wall" in the early '60s, before debuting as Stranger and Ken in 1963, with songs for Duke Reid ("Mow Sen Wa"), and Coxsone Dodd ("World's Fair"). Coxsone noticed Ken's soulful talents, and began directing him towards a solo career. In the sound war between Dodd and Reid, Ken became one of Studio One's big guns, along with former child star Delroy Wilson and Bajan soul man Jackie Opel.

This set kicks off with Sandie Shaw's 1967 Eurovision Song Contest winner, **Puppet On A String**; not perhaps the most promising material, but Ken transforms it into something more soulful, with some assured ad-libbing before the fade. A copy of the original arrived at the studio at the end of a session in spring 1967. Organist Jackie Mittoo heard the song, and ran after Ken, who had left the studio. Mittoo insisted he record it right away, and the musicians built a rugged rock steady rhythm in Studio One style, more aggressive than Duke Reid's sweeter variant; Ken's bravura pleading delivery ensured the tune was a big hit.

For the *Mr Rock Steady* album, issued in 1967, Coxsone augmented Ken's own dramatic compositions, like **My Heart Is Gone** and **Home, Home, Home**, with strong songs by top Jamaican writers. These included Bob Andy's bittersweet **I Don't Want To See You Cry**, Stranger Cole's classic **Give Me The Right** – a lovely duet with Norma Frazer – and Gaylad 'BB' Seaton's wistful **The Girl I Left Behind**. All were ideal for the young singer, who went on to top the UK charts in 1974 with his brilliant cover of "Everything I Own".

Ken showed early on that he could cover soul classics; on his third album, *More of Ken Boothe*, in 1969, he was to cut an excellent version of Fred Hughes' "Oo Wee Baby", and a remarkable tribute to Otis Redding with "Try A Little Tenderness". The fine interpretation of Sir Mack Rice's **Mustang Sally** included here amply demonstrates why he was often billed as "Jamaica's Wilson Pickett". This whole album is saturated in soul, whether it be the mutated doo-wop of **Give Me Back My Heart**, or Ken's interjections of "sock it to me" on **This Is Rock Steady**. It also proves conclusively that not only were Jamaican singers just as powerful as their US models, but rock steady was the perfect medium to carry that expression. This CD reissue adds two top-quality ska tracks – **Artibella** from 1963, and **Come Running Back** from 1965 – to the original album.

➲ We almost chose **Everything I Own**, Trojan, UK, 1989

Bounty Killer

My Xperience

TVT/VP Records, 1996, US

Recorded 1996. Bounty Killer (deejay). Features The Fugees, Barrington Levy, Junior Reid, Busta Rhymes, Raekwon, Beenie Man, Dennis Brown, Richie Stephens, Jeru Da Damaja, Sly & Robbie. Producers include Bounty Killer, Aden Jones, The Rza.

Over the course of the 1990s, the rockstone-voiced deejay Bounty Killer (born Rodney Price, in the ultra-rough Riverton City area of Kingston, in 1972) has seen off all the competition – with the single exception of his old rival Beenie Man. After receiving initial encouragement from his cousin, 1980s dancehall star John Wayne, he made his first record, as Bounty Hunter, in 1990, for King Jammy's brother Trevor 'Uncle T' James. "Gun Must Done", a promising enough generic effort, was quickly followed by a change of name and another single, "Dub Fi Dub". Not until he voiced "Spy Fi Die" for another member of Jammy's family, his son John John, however, did Bounty Killer gain his first real hit. Further best-sellers appeared on the various labels run by the James family, including "Roots, Reality & Culture", "Cellular Phone", "Book, Book, Book", "Miss Ivy Last Son" and "Smoke the Herb". Most were gathered on three classic deejay albums – *Jamaica's Most Wanted*, *Down In the Ghetto* and *No Argument*.

Bounty Killer's own Priceless label got off to a good start in 1995, but there came a period when one self-production after another failed to register with record buyers. However, by the late summer of 1997, Miss Ivy's last son was back with the brilliant "Tune In", on which he chatted over a remix of Sugar Minott's "Rub A Dub Sound" hit. It came to worldwide attention in the *Dancehall Queen* movie, and was followed by a sensational series of discs for Colin 'Bulby' York's Fat Eyes imprint, including "Cry & A Bawl" with the feisty Tanya Stephens.

The newcomer to Bounty Killer won't go far wrong with any of his albums, but the best starting point has to be the first over which he had total control. Released in 1996, **My Xperience** was obviously aimed at an international audience – as witnessed by guest spots from compatible hip-hoppers like Erik Sermon, the Fugees, Busta Rhymes, Raekwon and Blahzay Blahzay. Even so, Bounty Killer's imagination and self-assurance were unaffected, and he certainly didn't forget his dancehall followers. All these qualities ensured the complete success of all twenty tracks. The biggest relief to his original fans was probably that the numbers on which he was joined by US stars worked just as well as those with more predictable sparring partners – Junior Reid, Anthony Malvo and Anthony 'Red' Rose, Barrington Levy, Beenie Man and Dennis Brown, and Richie Stephens.

As with his previous sets, a generous portion of genuine reggae hits was included. Few tunes, for instance, were more popular in the London and New York reggae markets of late 1995, as well as Jamaica, than **Living Dangerously**, with the singer Barrington Levy. Another popular 'combination' tune, when first released as a single on the incredibly named How yu fi sey dat? label, was **Guns & Roses**, on which he commented on what the production team of Anthony 'Red' Rose and Anthony Malvo had to say. Bounty Killer even acquits himself well in tandem with Beenie Man over a remix of Dennis Brown's 1983 killer **Revolution**, which had previously notched up dancehall play and sales as a Fat Eyes 45, while a different mix of **Fed Up** was the major Jamaican hit on Taxi in 1996, as were **My Xperience** itself and **Ask Fi War** for the deejay's own Priceless label. Fresh material of the same scintillating calibre completes a true tour-de-force that has its feet firmly set in the dancehall, while looking far beyond.

➲ We almost chose **No Argument**, Greensleeves, UK, 1996

Dennis Brown

Some Like It Hot

Heartbeat, 1992, US

Recorded mid-1970s. Dennis Brown (vocals); backing includes Soul Syndicate and The Cimarons. Produced by Winston 'Niney' Holness (Niney The Observer).

Kingston-born Dennis Brown (1956–99) was brought up in a show business family: his father Arthur Brown was an actor-playwright; his uncle Basil a well-known comedian. As a ten-year-old, Dennis caused a sensation at the Carib Theatre and the National Arena, and in 1968, billed as the 'Wonder Boy', he appeared on stage shows all over Jamaica, notably on 'Smashville 68' supporting King Curtis and the Sweet Inspirations. He then joined Byron Lee's band.

It was when singing for Lee that Dennis Brown met up with producer Winston 'Niney' Holness, who encouraged him to try recording. He began at Studio One, singing backup on mentor Alton Ellis's *Sunday Coming* album, and recording a few songs on his own with Lloyd 'Matador' Daley and Derrick Harriott. However, it was when Niney took Dennis to Joe Gibbs's Kingston studio that he really took off as a singer, recording the first hit version of "Money In My Pocket" in 1972.

After Niney returned from a visit to England in 1973, he and Dennis began recording with the Soul Syndicate band. The first releases on his Observer label – Westbound Train and then Cassandra – were both huge hits. Niney conjured up a new sound on these records, built around Santa Davis's flying cymbal patterns and Earl 'Chinna' Smith's insinuating, propulsive guitar leads – a sound inspired by Al Green's band. This provided an ideal setting for Dennis's voice, an instrument equally capable of an intimate smoky warmth or a thrilling controlled power. They swept all before them in Jamaica that year, and in 1974 continued the style with tunes like the awesome **Conqueror** and **Ride On** – the latter with Big Youth. Best of all, perhaps, was **No More Will I Roam**, with Dennis incorporating a section of "Mas Que Nada" in his dramatic opening to the song. Brown also released the classic *Just Dennis* album in 1974.

The majority of the songs Dennis recorded with Niney were on roots and reality themes; when he did love songs, they were, as earlier in his career, generally covers, like the version of Ken Boothe's **You're No Good** on **Some Like It Hot** – which is essentially a Dennis Brown Greatest Hits. Other songs of this period, including the title track on this collection, **Some Like It Hot**, and **Yagga Yagga**, were recorded in London with the Cimarons in 1975 and then mixed in Jamaica. *Deep Down*, Brown's second Niney album, arrived at the end of the year.

By 1976, Dennis was firing with superb cultural songs, among them "Have No Fear" (here retitled **Here I Come**), "Whip Them Jah", and **Wolf And Leopards** (mixed at Black Ark by Lee Perry). But the Brown–Niney partnership was coming to an end and was not to be revived until the early 1990s.

Dennis subsequently became even more successful with, among others, Joe Gibbs, Sly & Robbie and his own DEB/Yvonne's labels, and, after a lean time during the digital years, he remained a successful singer until his death from "respiratory problems" in June, 1999. He was due to top the bill at the London Sunsplash, where he no doubt would have triumphed. But the Niney sessions of the 1970s were special. He and Dennis prepared to record by getting up at dawn and going to the beach. There they'd begin breathing exercises and swim. Afterwards, they'd cook ital stew, maybe smoke a chalice of herb, relax, sing and write songs. Then they'd go to the studio and build just one rhythm. Next day they would repeat the process, with Dennis adding his vocal. Twenty-five years on, the music still speaks volumes.

➲ We almost chose **Open The Gate**, Heartbeat, US, 1995

Glen Brown and King Tubby

Termination Dub 1973–79

Blood & Fire, 1996, UK

Recorded 1973–79. Glen Brown (producer; also gtr, kbds, pcn). Musicians include Aston Barrett (bass), Robbie Shakespeare (bass), Bobby Ellis (trpt), Vin Gordon (trbne), Tommy McCook (sax, flute), Carlton Barrett (drums), Carlton Davis (drums).

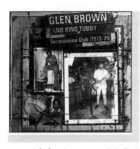

The musical career of Glen Brown began in Jamaica in the early 1960s, when he sang with the Sunny Bradshaw jazz group. As the decade moved on, he cut duets with Hopeton Lewis, Lloyd Robinson and Dave Barker, while in the early 1970s he recorded solo for Leslie Kong and Derrick Harriott. Brown's first shots at production came when he teamed up with businessman M.G. Mahtani for a series of distinctive 45s on the Shalimar label. The choppy rhythm employed on Gabby & the Rebels' "Only Love Can Make Me Smile" clearly anticipated similar ones that were to appear on Glen's own Pantomine (sic) and Dyer imprints, from 1972 onwards. Though Glen released some strong vocals on these labels, the deejay and instrumental versions attracted more attention. Later in the 1970s, Glen became less prolific, but adapted deftly to the new 'steppers' style, and built some of his hardest rhythms to support singers like Richard McDonald, Wayne Jarrett, Sylford Walker and Glenmore Richards, as well as his own underrated vocals.

Most of the Glen Brown productions on **Termination Dub**, as taken apart and reassembled by King Tubby, are drawn from this era of militant 'steppers'. However, his association with Tubby went back further. Tubby's initial experiments were for sound system play only, but Glen had been one of the first producers to have this extraordinary engineer remix his tracks for commercial release. The manner in which Tubby reconstructed those early tracks made them among the most radical of their time. By the time the cuts here were recorded, the Dub Master had handed over most of the mixing duties to his various apprentices, but he still sat at the mixing board when sufficiently interested – which he invariably was with Glen's music.

Termination Dub itself, which opens the album, is the oldest track, a hitherto unreleased version of a rhythm best known through two of the few Jamaican hits Glen has enjoyed – Tommy McCook and Rad Wilson's horns classic, "Dirty Harry", and deejay Prince Jazzbo's "Mr. Harry Skank". This prime treatment from King Tubby easily lives up to its lineage, and stands as further proof that a great rhythm can be versioned any number of times – so long as imagination on the Tubby scale is involved. After that, the listener is treated to a lesson in how Tubby's brilliance hadn't dimmed in the slightest.

Employing echo and reverb effects to full advantage, these are exemplary Tubby mixes. Anyone fortunate enough to know the originals will need no encouragement to hear the dubs of classics like Glenmore Richards's "Save Our Nation", Sylford Walker's "Eternal Day", Wayne Jarrett's "Youthman" or Glen's own "Forward the Good". Perhaps the best demonstration of the variety Tubby could bring lies in the two different versions to Walker's "Cleanliness Is Godliness", which are segued together. Both titled **Assack Lawn No 1 Dub** when they appeared on alternate pressings of the single, the first keeps several snatches of the vocal, as well as the inspired horns line, while the second mix drops the singer completely, retains less of the horns, and for the most part allows the raw rhythm to run. Hearing Glen's rhythms reduced to their component parts should have many who are new to them searching for all the other cuts. At the moment, the only way of finding any of them on CD is the superb Sylford Walker set given as our alternative choice below and which includes his "Lamb's Bread", "Cleanliness Is Godliness" and "Eternal Day".

➲ We almost chose **Sylford Walker: Chant Down...**, Shanachie, US, 1989

Burning Spear

Marcus Garvey

Island, 1975, UK/US; re-released on CD with *Garvey's Ghost*

Recorded 1974. Burning Spear: Winston Rodney (vocals), Delroy Hines (vocals), Rupert Willington (vocals). Musicians include Earl Smith (gtr), Tony Chin (gtr), Aston Barrett (bass), Robbie Shakespeare (bass), Bobby Ellis (trumpet), Vin Gordon (trombone), Carlton Samuels (flute), Leroy Wallace (drums). Produced by Jack Ruby.

Like so many of his predecessors, Burning Spear started out at Studio One. Born Winston Rodney in 1948, in St Ann's Bay, he took his performing name from Kenya's founder Jomo Kenyatta – which means 'burning spear' in Swahili – and began recording at Coxsone's Brentford Road studio. In 1969, working as a duo with Rupert Willington, under the aegis of singer Larry Marshall, he cut classics like "Door Peeper" and "Zion Higher". Released as singles in the UK on the Bamboo/Banana labels, they met with little success; after the label folded in 1971, they could be found in Tesco supermarkets for ten pence.

In the early Seventies, the UK-led reggae market was dominated by more commercial sounds. Spear's roots style, like that of the Ethiopians and the Abyssinians, was regarded as deeply esoteric. Spear stayed with Dodd until 1974, recording enough material for two whole albums – *Studio One Presents Burning Spear* and *Rocking Time* – and several singles. The nearest he came to a hit was in 1972, when the rhythm track to "He Prayed" became a big sound system favourite, and was versioned by Big Youth for his commentary on the George Foreman–Joe Frazier fight, which took place in Kingston.

By 1974, Spear had added another backing vocalist, Delroy Hines, and the trio began to record for the Ocho Rios-based sound system owner Jack Ruby (aka Lawrence Lindo). Ruby was an excellent producer; for the sessions at Randy's Studio 17 in downtown Kingston, he assembled a superb band, including a five-man horn section.

The sound they made was brooding, deep, and above all, heavy. It perfectly underscored Spear's lyrics, which dealt with serious subjects – the colonial history of Jamaica, the role of Pan-Africanist Marcus Mosiah Garvey, and personal and social redemption – that were far removed from reggae's usual perceived concerns. All this was delivered in a vocal style that ranged from a husky emotive plea to an hypnotic mantra-like chant that soared freely over the sonorous horn charts.

Selections from **Marcus Garvey** were heavily previewed on Jamaican and UK sound systems, and built up a considerable underground following. When Jack Ruby released the singles **Marcus Garvey** and **Slavery Days** in the summer of 1975, soon followed by the album itself, they sold very well, and not only to the roots audience. Island Records signed a deal with Ruby and Spear, and released *Marcus Garvey* – slightly speeded up and with one extra track (**Resting Place**) – in the UK, where it immediately gained the sort of attention in the mainstream rock press previously claimed only by Bob Marley and the Wailers. *Garvey's Ghost*, a rather dry dub version of the album, was also released, mixed at Island Studios in London by Ruby himself; it is included on the CD reissue.

Spear's next three studio albums – *Man In The Hills* (1976), *Dry & Heavy* (1977) and *Marcus Children* aka *Social Living* (1978), augmented the vision of *Marcus Garvey* and significantly reworked major portions of his earlier Coxsone output. These sets remain the cornerstone of all his subsequent work, which has continued with remarkable consistency right up to the present. *Marcus Garvey* was the set that presented that vision first; if ever an album deserved the title epochal, this is it.

➲ We almost chose **Social Living**, 1978 Blood & Fire, UK, 1994

Bushman

Nyah Man Chant

Greensleeves, 1997, UK

Recorded 1997. Bushman (vocals). Musicians include Dean Fraser (tenor sax), Nambo Robinson (trombone), Chico Chin (horns), Earl 'Chinna' Smith (gtr). Produced by Steely & Clevie.

Born Dwight Duncan in 1973, and raised at Prospect Beach on Jamaica's East Coast, where he was brought up in the Rasta faith, Bushman delivered one of the strongest debuts in many a year with 1997's **Nyah Man Chant**. He can sound like Dennis Brown or Luciano – whom he cites, with Marley, as major influences – but here he also uses his 'own' voice, a husky, resonant baritone. He started singing in his local church choir at the age of nine; by his early teens, he had adopted the name Junior Melody, and he later called himself Junior Buckley.

The youth gained his first experience of the reggae business selecting for a sound system called Black Star Line, where his colleagues advised him to sing rather than deejay. With no studio in the vicinity, taking his career to the next level – making a record – meant hitch-hiking seventy miles to Kingston. Even there, it was no easy task to gain the ear of a suitable producer. However, in 1997, Bushman was lucky enough to link up with Steely and Clevie, who happened one day to be playing football in the car park at the famous dub-cutting studio 'Arrows' on Windward Road. He auditioned on the spot, and Steely invited him down to Studio 2000.

Both Bushman's first two singles for Steely & Clevie – chanting style on **Grow Your Natty**, bleakly lyrical on **Call The**

Hearse – rode hardcore dancehall rhythms. These were followed by **Remember The Days**, expressing a desire for the togetherness of old-school style dancehall, delivered over an r'n'b vamp. The 'friends' to which it was also credited – Skatta, Dellie Ranks and Benjie Myaz, the underrated female singer Sharon Forrester, and the very capable deejays Don Yute and Daddy Screw – all got a chance to feature.

On the next single, the focus was totally on Bushman. **Black Star Liner** brought him wider attention, and changed the direction of his career, as he told John Masouri in *Echoes* in August 1997: "After that tune . . . Steelie and Clevie . . . start say 'Well, that youth there, them faster riddim definitely not for him.' A one-drop them need fi me, so then we start mek that happen".

The single – and the brilliant **Man A Lion** – sold well, in the UK particularly. Although Bushman was scarcely known, the album that followed, *Nyah Man Chant*, enjoyed a positive critical reaction. Steely and Clevie's sympathetic production, with great use of real horns, along with string samples and hardcore beats, contributed significantly to its artistic success.

The whole album is a coherent, excellently crafted set. Other highlights include **My Day**, which adapts the soul tune "Our Day Will Come" by Ruby and the Romantics, converting the lyric to a Rasta viewpoint and using the "Necktie" rhythm, the scathing **Poor People Power**, over Steely and Clevie's cut of the "Heptones Gonna Fight" rhythm, and **Rude Boy Life**, more chilling reportage along the lines of "Call The Hearse".

Bushman took a break after Greensleeves released the album, returning in late 1998 and early 1999 with fine singles for Bobby Digital, Winston Riley, and Lloyd 'Pickout' Dennis. The promise of the first album was maintained on his second, for King Jammy (see below), although that had slightly more conventional production values and Bushman's influences were, if anything, more evident. Hopefully he will progress further; in the meantime, *Nyah Man Chant* is as good an example of modern roots singing as you could hope to find.

⮞ We almost chose **Total Commitment**, Greensleeves, UK, 1999

Prince Buster

King of Ska

Quattro, 1992, Japan

Recorded 1962–66. Prince Buster All Stars, including Arkland 'Drumbago' Parks (drums), Stanley 'Ribbs' Notice (sax), Oswald 'Baba' Brooks (trumpet). Also features Don Drummond (trombone), Val Bennett (sax), Lester Sterling (sax), Jackie Mittoo (organ). Produced by Prince Buster.

The contribution made by Prince Buster to the development of Jamaican music was immense. The diminutive Prince was born Cecil Campbell, on May 28, 1938, in the rough Luke Lane area of downtown Kingston. A former boxer, he started in the music business collecting the gate money at Coxsone dances in the '50s, and became the first true-born ghetto man producer.

His entry into production came about when Duke Reid asked him to stand in during a temporary absence. According to singer Derrick Morgan, of the twelve tunes Buster recorded, he gave one to Duke and kept the rest for himself, including hits such as "30 Pieces Of Silver". By 1960 he had cut "Oh Carolina" with the Folkes Brothers and Count Ossie. Buster was among the first to look to Jamaica for new sounds to replace American r'n'b, asking his musicians – guitarist Jah Jerry and pianist Theo 'Easy Snappin' Beckford – to emphasize the 'afterbeat' of the first and third beats of the traditional r'n'b measure. That became the defining rhythmic signature of ska.

By 1961, Buster was recording 'proto-ska' – the stressed after-beat is first heard on Eric Morris's "Humpty Dumpty" and Buster's own "They Got To Go", directed to his rivals in the dancehall. A year later, the motif can be heard in full effect – on piano, guitar and horns – on songs like the scorching Madness.

Over the next few years, Buster made some of the greatest ska; much has never been reissued. This Japanese CD, **King of Ska**, begins that task with sixteen prime tracks. Only a handful feature Buster's vocals, including "Madness", the rollicking Enjoy Yourself, and Fire Stick, which draws on Jamaican folklore.

The instrumentals are the cream here, from the driving minor-key Downbeat Burial and Super Charge, with tenor saxophonists Dennis 'Ska' Campbell (no relation) and Val Bennett honking on the afterbeat in fine style, to Roland Alphonso's jazz-ska recasting of Lerner and Loewe's Almost Like Being In Love. At least four tunes have never been released before – Jack The Ripper, Count Machuki, Beat Street Jump, and Forresters Hall. All the top musicians played for Buster. As well as his own All Stars, he also used the Skatalites – Don Drummond contributes a pithy solo to "Mr Prince", while the adventurous Seven Wonders Of The World is a striking precursor of the 'far east sound' of the 1970s, with brilliant organ by Jackie Mittoo, and blistering Drummond trombone.

Apart from a few forays into mid-'70s 'rockers', Prince Buster stopped producing by 1971; in the 1960s, however, he was the man. He had international links early on, through his connection to indie entrepreneur Emil Shalit's Blue Beat label, which issued over 600 Buster productions in the UK. Buster toured the UK and met the Beatles; he later became a Black Muslim, and mixed with Malcolm X and Muhammad Ali. By the early '70s he had had enough, stating that "They have used guns to spoil the fun and force tasteless and meaningless music upon the land." However, he occasionally tours even today, gaining a strong following among 'new-ska' devotees.

Unbelievably, this is the only legal compilation of his work that is currently available. Fortunately it is superb, with master tape sound quality and excellent selections. In the absence of a Prince Buster CD box set, it is unreservedly recommended.

➲ This is it on CD for Prince Buster

Junior Byles

Curly Locks: The Best of Junior Byles & The Upsetters 1970–1976

Heartbeat, 1997, US

Recorded 1970–76. Junior Byles (vocals) with The Upsetters. Produced by Lee Perry.

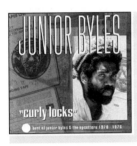

The most inspired and anguished of the singers associated with the 'rebel music' phase of the early 1970s, Junior Byles was born to a devout family in Kingston in 1948. The intense spirituality that infuses his work can be traced to his early years, singing in church. His entry into the record business came in 1967 when he formed the Versatiles with Louie Davis and Dudley Earl, who recorded initially for Joe Gibbs. The man who supervised their debut session, however, was Lee 'Scratch' Perry, who was soon to strike out on his own. Byles and Scratch's professional relationship was to yield some of the most impressive tunes in the careers of both men. In the same period Byles recorded a couple of fine records for his own Love Power imprint. Between 1974 and 1977, he made further striking sides – almost all from a 'sufferer's' perspective – for Pete Weston, Channel One, Dudley Swaby, Lloyd F. Campbell, Niney and Joe Gibbs. Just as the Rasta-inspired themes he helped to popularize found an international audience, however, his recording activities were unfortunately curtailed by his worsening mental condition.

The earlier of the two stints with Scratch covered on **Curly Locks** coincided with the Wailers' mould-shattering work with the producer, and featured the same set of musicians, supplying similarly tough sinewy rhythms, at Randy's Studio 17. The later sessions took place in 1974, when Perry set up his own Black Ark studio, and was working with an entirely different band. The sound that then emerged was even denser and 'dreader'. An example of the first approach is the oldest track here, a previously unreleased cut of **What's the World Coming To**, lacking the strings that spoiled the UK single. Another is Byles' entry for the 1972 Festival Song Competition, **Da Da**, which shows him in wonderfully exuberant mood. One of the set's seven previously unissued tracks follows: an alternative cut with different lyrics, lasting over six minutes. Among the released rarities from this period is Byles' significantly remoulded interpretation of Little Willie John's **Fever**, supplemented by a deejay cut from Jah T, over Augustus Pablo's melodica version.

An even more compelling early record is **A Place Called Africa**, one of the most sublime pleas for repatriation ever recorded. Like many of the best tracks from 1972 and 1973, it found its way onto the seminal *Beat Down Babylon* album. Here it's followed by the Dennis Alcapone version, one of the deejay's best performances. Two more contenders for Byles' greatest-ever achievement are from the second phase. Both **Long Way** and **Curly Locks** show the early Black Ark sound at its finest. The slow rhythm of the former perfectly underscores a lyric ostensibly about his relationship with a women, which can just as easily be given a 'cultural' reading; the latter, always a favourite with the UK 'lovers' audience, also has a roots slant, as Byles pleads his case with a girl whose father disapproves of his dreadlocks.

Whether this collection lives up to its title is a moot point. After all, it misses the record that established Byles – his biggest Jamaican hit, "Beat Down Babylon" – substituting **Informer Man**, on the same rhythm. A pity the listener couldn't have been treated to both. There are also a couple of weak tracks, while important tunes like "Pharaoh Hiding", "Joshua's Desire", "Rasta No Pickpocket", and "Auntie Lulu" are missing. But these are small quibbles when considering the general quality of what is present.

➲ We almost chose **129 Beat Street**, Blood & Fire, UK, 1998

The Cables

What Kind Of World

Studio One, 1970, JA; Heartbeat, 1991, US.

Recorded 1970. The Cables (Keeble Drummond, Elbert Stewart and Vince Stoddart); with Sound Dimension and others.

Arguably the most under-valued of all the great Jamaican vocal-harmony trios, The Cables were never prolific, but their limited body of work deserves comparison with the best of the more widely acclaimed Heptones, Paragons and Melodians. The group began by recording "Good Luck To You" for Sonia Pottinger, before making their initial impact on the Jamaican charts of 1968 with **Baby Why** for Clement Dodd.

Perhaps because Coxsone was enjoying considerable success with a plethora of gifted acts, including the Heptones, Ken Boothe and Bob Andy, they were not given as much attention at Studio One as they deserved, having to take something of a back seat when it came to recording over the new-style rhythms being cut. Yet their position in the pecking order of the day was always belied by the impeccable quality of everything they cut at Brentford Road – little more than the contents of this one album, **What Kind Of World**.

Afterwards, they cut fine discs for 'Sir' J.J. Johnson and Harry Johnson, as well as the 'revive' favourite "A Sometime Girl" for the obscure Electro label. That the trio did not record more – just one album for Harry Johnson followed this classic debut – is testimony to the sheer amount of vocal talent then available for the studio bosses to pick. Certainly there was no faulting the aching lead vocals of Keeble Drummond, after whom the group took their name, or the assured harmonies of Elbert Stewart and Vince Stoddart. The smooth, soulful sound created by the Cables' blend of voices was very much that of a classic rock steady trio. It just so happened that they sang for Dodd as newer, more emphatic rhythms were being developed by his session musicians.

The ten steadfast rhythms employed here are another reason why this short set belongs in every reggae collection. The Jackie Mittoo-arranged one employed for **Baby Why** left a virtual history of reggae in its wake. It was given deejay treatments by the contrasting talents of Dennis Alcapone and Prince Jazzbo, and when the roots era dawned in 1974, the Gladiators' "Re-arrange" fitted the rhythm just as well; then the following year one of the tunes that established the Channel One 'rockers' approach, the Mighty Diamonds' "Have Mercy", employed a more streamlined updating, as did the next version from the hottest deejay of the day, Trinity, while Dodd answered back with a back-to-basics cut on the Bionic Dub album. The Cables recut the song for Harry Johnson at the close of the decade (and were again joined by Jazzbo for the 12-inch mix).

There were never quite as many cuts of the Cables' other important Jamaican hit, **What Kind Of World**, though a dub cut surfaced on the same Bionic Dub set, and Sugar Minott impressed a few years later with another wonderful vocal, "Change Your Ways". **Be A Man** uses the same rhythm as Larry Marshall's "Can't You Understand" and was only treated to one subsequent chapter from Studio One: a track on Sample Dub. But it remains a mystery why just as strong tracks like **My Broken Heart** and **Love Is A Pleasure** have remained unplundered for further versions.

Perhaps when these tracks, too, have been rediscovered by Jamaican producers, this most perfect of Studio One vocal albums will finally receive its due recognition.

⮑ We almost chose **Gaylads/Soul Beat**, Studio One, US, 1997

22

Capleton

Prophecy

Def Jam/Ral/African Star, 1995, US

Recorded 1994–95. Capleton (deejay). Producers: Richard Bell, Colin York and Linford Marshall, Jonathan 'Lil Jon' Smith and Paul Lewis, Stuart Brown.

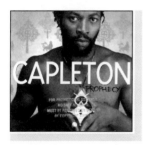

Now one of the leading 'Bobo Dread' chanters, the deejay Capleton (born Clifton Bailey in Kingston in 1974) first came to public attention in 1990. On "Number One On the Look Good Chart", he 'bigged up' the female populations of several countries – including Russia! Over a fresh-sounding cut of the then-omnipresent "Punaany" rhythm from the New York production team of Hyman Wright and Percy Chin, Capleton found himself with a major hit in Kingston, London and New York.

The new kid on the block went on to earn a reputation as one of the slackest deejays around. Titles like "The Red" (Jammy's), "Rough Rider" (Uncle T), and "Bumbo Red" (Xterminator) left little to the imagination, while demonstrating he certainly knew how to ride a rhythm with aplomb. Interspersed with these hardcore tunes were some incisive 'reality' cuts that looked to the future – most notably "Too Warsome" (Fresh Breed), "God Mi Love, We Nuh Love Satan" (Bravo the Best Baby Father) and "Ghetto Youth" (Black Scorpio). Even "Gun Talk'" (Jammy's) was as much a warning to the gun-crazy ghetto youth of West Kingston as the usual bad boy braggadocio.

The major shift in Capleton's attitude, however, came about in 1992, when he enjoyed two massive hits with 'cultural' themes – 'Almshouse' for Philip 'Fatis' Burrell, and "The Prophet" for

Donovan Germain, followed by the almost as successful "Mankind" for Colin 'Fatta' Walters. These seemed to point the way forward, as Capleton then openly declared his Rastafarian beliefs, and has concentrated almost entirely ever since on lyrics informed by his faith.

During the last half-dozen years, Capleton has been chiefly associated with Stuart Brown's Jamaican sound system and record label African Star, which specializes in cultural lyrics over progressive dancehall rhythms. **Tour**, which kicks off **Prophecy**, was a vintage sufferer's tune for the label that became a massive reggae seller in 1994. Capleton's next cut of the rhythm, "Chalice" – not on this set – was more significant still; its additional nyahbingi drumming became fashionable in 1995, when Bobby Digital put out countless versions of his "Kette Drum" rhythm. While continuing to record for African Star, Capleton also found time to cut just as unremittingly cultural tunes for other labels, including Star Trail, Fat Eyes and Mixing Lab.

Prophecy, Capleton's first uncompromisingly conscious album for the US hip-hop imprint Defjam, with whom he signed in 1995, bears comparison with Buju Banton's classic *'Til Shiloh*, released that same year. All fifteen tracks demonstrate just how serious modern ragga deejays can be, and make up a wall-to-wall declaration of the teachings Capleton received from the Bobo Dread followers of the late Prince Emmanuel Edwards. Included are several former African Star singles – **Wings Of the Morning**, **Obstacle** and **Babylon Judgment**, as well as the anthemic "Tour". To ensure variety, some memorable moments with other producers have also been slotted in – **Don't Diss the Trinity** from Richard Bell, **Heathen Reign** from Roy Francis, and **No Competition** from Colin 'Bulby' York and Linford 'Fatta' Marshall – plus three hip-hop remixes, including one of "Tour", from Jonathan 'Lil Jon' Smith and Paul Lewis. The one album Capleton has released since, 1997's *I Testament*, is slightly disappointing, but subsequent singles, on African Star and other labels, show that both his beliefs and talent remain intact.

➲ We almost chose **Good So**, VP Records, US, 1995

Johnny Clarke

Dreader Dread 1976–78

Blood & Fire, 1998, UK

Recorded 1976–78. Johnny Clarke (vocals). Produced by Johnny Clarke and Bunny Lee.

The young Johnny Clarke, who was born in Kingston in 1955, was producer Bunny 'Striker' Lee's most prolific singer during the 1970s. He scored with roots anthems and love songs, his own lyrics and 'do overs' – new versions of old lyrics – which included not only the Studio One classics that everyone was versioning, but also the repertoire of cultural artists like Bob Marley, the Abyssinians, Culture and the Mighty Diamonds. Virgin quite appositely titled their first Clarke album *Authorised Version*. In Jamaica, Clarke was at least as popular as Dennis Brown and Gregory Isaacs, but both his extremely prolific output for Striker, and his penchant for versioning other singers' hits, worked against his crossing over to the wider international audience he deserved.

After a few early records for Clancy Eccles, Rupie Edwards – "Everyday You Wondering" was the original cut of Edwards' UK pop hit "Irie Feeling" – and Keith Hudson associate Stamma, Clarke started to record for Bunny Lee in 1974. At the time, Lee was picking up on the prominent use of the high hat in US disco records, and encouraging his drummer, Carlton 'Santa' Davis, to develop what became known as the 'flying cymbals' sound. Clarke's hits during this phase began with "None Shall Escape the Judgment", originally cut for Striker by the Greenwich Park rootsman Earl Zero, and continued with the self-written "Move Out Of Babylon Rastaman", "Enter Into His Gates With Praise" and "Jah Jah Bless Joshua", along with an inspired version of Delano Stewart's "Rock With Me Baby", probably the best of his non-cultural tunes.

Unusually, Johnny Clarke did not then begin a frantic round of freelancing with different producers. Instead he stayed almost totally loyal to Striker well into the second half of the 1970s, as the rhythms heard in Kingston's dancehalls shifted to a new more militant feel. This extremely fruitful period in his career is the focus of the **Dreader Dread** collection, which mostly consists of singles from Bunny Lee labels such as Jackpot, Justice and Attack, together with one that appeared on Clarke's own Lion Rock imprint.

Clearly neither producer or singer found it hard to adapt to the heavyweight 'steppers' rhythms that were now ruling the dancehalls. They proceeded to notch up a considerable number of sizeable hits, several of which are included here. The self-produced **African People**, for instance, is chronologically the earliest track – released in January, 1976 – but is underpinned by a rhythm as hard as anything that followed. The common African heritage of all black people was a popular topic in the 1970s, but the combination of a killer rhythm and Clarke's appealing tone lift both this and the slightly later **African Roots** far above most similar tunes. Similarly the apocalyptic sentiments on **Every Knee Shall Bow** or **Fire And Brimstone A Go Burn the Wicked** may not be exactly original, but once again they seem entirely convincing when sung by Clarke, as though confirming age-old truths.

While most of the material is Clarke's own, a couple of his trademark 'do overs' of other singers' hits are also included. Justifiably so; rather than routine covers, his cuts of both Peter Tosh's "I'm the Toughest" (as **Top Ranking**) and Marley's **Time Will Tell** stand as genuinely fresh reinterpretations, and are as rough as anything recorded by the singer who pointed the way towards the 'dancehall' phase of the music.

⊃ We almost chose **Meets Barry Brown**, Fatman, UK, 1996

Cocoa Tea

Israel's King

VP Records, 1996, US

Musicians include Sly Dunbar, Dean Frazer and Donald Dennis. Produced by Phillip 'Fatis' Burrell.

One of the most consistent singers in Jamaican music and blessed with a voice as sweet as his name indicates, Cocoa Tea (born Calvin George Scott; Rocky Point, Clarendon, 1959) has never really had his due as an international reggae star. And yet he has more claims than most to be a successor to Bob Marley, as **Israel's King**, his fourth set for producer Phillip 'Fatis' Burrell, nicely demonstrates.

Calvin began singing at school in Clarendon, and – like so many great Jamaican vocalists – in church choirs. He recorded his first single at age 14 for producer Willie Francis. When it flopped, the youth followed his other interest, horse racing, becoming a jockey for a few years, and also worked as a fisherman. He continued to sing with sound systems in his area, however, and after the birth of his first child, Rashane, decided to make music his full-time career. Early in 1984, as Cocoa Tea, he hooked up with producer Henry 'Junjo' Lawes and had a string of hits including "I Lost My Sonia", "Rocking Dolly" and "Evening Time". Over the next few years he recorded for most of the top producers. His output included a pair of albums apiece for Micky 'Pep' Chin, King Jammy, and Augustus 'Gussie' Clarke. He scored big hits for the latter pair on combination tracks featuring him alongside deejay Shabba Ranks or Cutty Ranks and vocal group Home T.

For Mikey Bennett, he was also pretty convincing on a trio of records about the Gulf War, as well as on the anti-firearms "Gun Ting". Then in the late 1980s Cocoa Tea began an association with former Jammy engineer Bobby Digital, hitting with love songs ("Love Me Truly") and, in the early '90s, with roots material. In 1991 Cocoa Tea was number one in the reggae chart with "Rikers Island', an adaptation of John Holt's 1976 hit "Up Park Camp", recorded for the New York-based Mr Doo label. His brilliant "Good Life" – riding an update of the "Party Time" rhythm – was one of the biggest hits of 1994.

By 1995 Cocoa Tea had become a fully committed Rastaman, and his version of Bob Marley's "Heathen" for Bobby Digital that year spawned a whole album on the rhythms. His work for Fatis was no less rootsy, particularly on albums like 1993's *One Up* and 1996's *Israel's King*. *Israel's King* is perhaps the best of all his sets for Fatis; the overall sound, with a four-girl backing chorus, suggests what Bob Marley might have sounded like had he lived, although many reckon Cocoa Tea's voice superior.

Lyrically the album is mostly Rasta-informed roots and reality. As well as the more customary repatriation plaints and praises for Jah – Repatriation, Israel's King – he takes social themes and links them intelligently with his Rasta beliefs: domestic violence, for example, on Bruck Loose, or police informers on the powerful Rastaman. Cocoa Tea also does a (solitary) love song, Don't Want To Live Without Your Love – a gentle lovers rock. Musically, the whole album is propelled by dynamic and assured rhythms built by Sly Dunbar, Firehouse's Donald Dennis and Dean Frazer. Obvious highlights include the duet with Luciano on Rough Inna Town and the beautiful Hurry Up And Come.

Cocoa Tea has long professed an aim to be a role model like his own inspiration Bob Marley; his latest enterprise was setting up his own label, Roaring Lion. Not yet 40, he looks set to continue well into the next millennium.

⟳ We almost chose **Sweet Sweet Cocoa Tea**, Cornerstone, US, 1999

The Congos

Heart of the Congos

Black Ark, 1977, JA; Blood & Fire, 1996, UK

Recorded 1976–77. The Congos: Cedric Myton (vcls), Roydel 'Ashanti' Johnson (vcls), Watty 'King' Burnett (vcls). Backing vocalists include Gregory Isaacs, the Heptones, and the Meditations. Produced by Lee Perry.

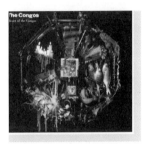

Originally a duo of Cedric Myton and Roydel 'Ashanti' Johnson, the Congos were joined for their one classic album, the Lee 'Scratch' Perry production **Heart of the Congos**, by Black Ark stalwart Watty 'King' Burnett. Cedric was born in 1947 in St Catherine. His career went back to the late '60s, when he sang with Devon Russell, 'Prince' Lincoln Thompson and Lindberg 'Preps' Lewis on the Tartans' "Dance All Night" on Merritone Records, as well as "Coming On Strong" for Caltone and "Far Beyond the Sun" for Treasure Isle. After the Tartans split up, Cedric continued to record with Devon, and he also linked up with Lincoln Thompson's Royal Rasses in the mid-'70s, for the roots classics "Kingston 11" and "Love the Way It Should Be".

Roydel Johnson (born 1947, Hanover, Jamaica) had sung with several Rastafarian ensembles, including Ras Michael and the Sons of Negus, while Watty Burnett had recorded for Scratch both as a solo singer and with Clinton 'Tony' Fearon of the Gladiators. Together as the Congos, the three singers were responsible for the most fully realized of all the albums recorded at Scratch's Black Ark studio in its six years of operation.

The complete aesthetic success of the set was not simply the result of Perry's having perfected his use of the studio he was soon to destroy. While the sound – involving the deployment of Echoplex reverb unit, Mutron phaser and Soundcraft board – was breathtaking in its multi-layered density, the vocal talents with whom he was working were of equal importance.

The interplay between the falsetto of Cedric Myton and the tenor of Roydel Johnson would have been enough under most circumstances, but Scratch chose to utilize comparable talents for the backing vocals – the baritone of Watty Burnett, plus the harmonies of Barry Llewelyn and Earl Morgan from the Heptones, Gregory Isaacs, the Meditations, and Candy McKenzie from Full Experience.

Heart of the Congos is an unparalleled showcase of Jamaican vocal technique. Just hear Watty Burnett dropping down to bass in praise of the collie man on **Fisherman**, to complete the full range of male voices, or how Ansel Cridland, Danny Clarke and Winston Watson of the Meditations add an extra richness to tracks like **Open The Gate** and **Solid Foundation**. Both Gregory Isaacs and the two Heptones make distinctive contributions to **La La Bam Bam**, while Candy McKenzie adds yet another vocal texture to the beautiful **Children Crying**.

For these sessions, Perry's studio band were at the peak of their powers. Particularly worth singling out are the percussion work of Uziah 'Sticky' Thompson, the veteran singer Noel 'Skully' Simms and Scratch himself, along with Ernest Ranglin's guitar, Winston Wright's organ, Boris Gardiner's bass, and the drums of Sly Dunbar and Mikey 'Boo' Richards.

The original vinyl album had a curious history. It was not picked up by Island, who had released Perry's own *Super Ape*, along with impressive albums from Max Romeo, the Heptones, George Faith and Jah Lloyd. Instead it appeared initially in two limited pressings on Scratch's Black Art imprint, each with a different mix, and there were three subsequent re-presses on different labels. On CD, this gem of Rasta-inspired harmonies is slightly longer than ever, and even more essential for including another disc's worth of dub and 12-inch versions.

➲ We almost chose **The Heptones: Party Time**, Island, UK, 1992

26

Lord Creator

Don't Stay Out Late

VP/Randy's, 1996, US

Recorded 1962–68. Lord Creator (vocals); musicians include the Skatalites.
Produced by Vincent 'Randy' Chin.

There's a strong case for saying that the greatest of all the ballad singers ever to record in Kingston was not a Jamaican at all, but the Trinidadian Lord Creator, who was born Kentrick Patrick around 1940. As befits his nom-de-disque and place of origin, Lord Creator started out singing calypso. His initial Jamaican hit was recorded on his home island, and it was the Caribbean-wide popularity of his first cut of **Evening News** that brought Creator to Jamaica. The hit was neither a love song nor calypso, but a poignant ballad about a ragged boy trying to make a living selling newspapers on the street.

Having made Jamaica his home in 1962, Lord Creator recorded music of the highest calibre for both Randy's and Studio One, including recuts of "Evening News". It was while he was performing at the Havana club in East Kingston that Creator's sophisticated style came to the attention of producer Vincent 'Randy' Chin. The British colony was then about to be granted independence, and Chin suggested that the young singer write a song in celebration. **Independent Jamaica** not only became one of the biggest hits of 1962 in Jamaica, but was fittingly the first release on Chris Blackwell's Island imprint in the UK. In common with all of Creator's material, it was sung in the clearest of dictions, displaying the influence of great American crooners like Nat 'King' Cole. But if Lord Creator always excelled with smooth ballads, he was no slouch when tackling either calypso or steaming ska tracks. His full range is displayed on the stunning **Don't Stay Out Late** compilation, which gathers everything he recorded for Chin in the 1960s.

Creator's melodic take on ska is typified by **Don't Stay Out Late** and **Man To Man**, on which he's accompanied by the same musicians who, as the Skatalites, cut blistering instrumentals like "Malcolm X" and "Sam the Fisherman" for Chin. Looking further back to his Trinidadian roots, **Ma & Pa** is essentially calypso, though it's obviously the same musicians behind him. Besides possessing one of the finest voices ever to grace a Kingston recording session, Creator was probably the finest songwriter working in Jamaica during this period. The beautiful **We Will Be Lovers**, which was massive in 1963, apparently came about when Norma Fraser asked him to write a song for her and then had difficulties handling it in the studio. She suggested Creator sing the song with her, but as it turned out it was a case of Norma singing with him – he takes the lead throughout.

Lord Creator's most successful song of all time was "Kingston Town", recorded at the end of the 1960s for Clancy Eccles; a progenitor appears here in the form of **King & Queen (Babylon)**. "Kingston Town" sold well in the UK without ever charting, but twenty years later it became an international hit for the pop-reggae band UB40, and some very welcome royalty cheques meant that Creator was able to buy a house.

Such Is Life is the 1968 original cut of a song he was later to record for Lee Perry: the very different production styles make both versions essential Lord Creator. **Come Down 68**, with its lyric about longing for his woman while spending the night in jail, was recorded the same year, at a time when Creator was in danger of being forgotten by a new generation of record buyers and producers. But all the sides gathered here are among the most moving ever to emerge from a Kingston studio, and quite unlike what anyone else was doing then – or since.

➲ We almost chose **Golden Love**, Studio One, US, 1998

27

Culture

Trod On

Heartbeat, 1993, US/UK

Recorded 1979. Culture: Joseph Hill (vocals), Kenneth Paley (vocals), Albert Walker (vocals). Features Sly & Robbie and Count Ossie. Produced by Sonia Pottinger.

Culture – lead singer Joseph Hill, plus backing vocalists Albert Walker (Joseph's cousin) and Kenneth Dayes (aka Kenneth Paley, Albert's cousin) – are justly famed for the brilliant Garveyite prophecy song "Two Sevens Clash". That was their first hit, recorded in 1976 for producer Joe Gibbs, and showpiece of a hugely popular album. But the songs they made with Mrs Sonia Pottinger, collected on **Trod On**, show the original trio in a more consistently realized form.

Hill cut some sides at Studio One with the fine Linstead-based band, the Soul Defenders, in the early 1970s, which are now available on the Heartbeat CD *Soul Defenders at Studio One*. He then sang in hotel bands until early 1976, when Walker suggested they form a group. At first they called themselves the African Disciples, but they became Culture when they linked up with Gibbs. He put them to work under the supervision of Morris 'Blacka' Morwell, at that time responsible for running sessions in Gibbs' Retirement Crescent studio, where they made enough material for three albums. *Two Sevens Clash*, *Baldhead Bridge* and *Culture* were all issued by Gibbs, but although they achieved instant recognition with the hit, the relationship was not to last.

Culture went on to record an album at Harry J Studio, which was subsequently released without their permisssion as *Africa Stand Alone*, then quickly re-recorded all the songs for Mrs

Pottinger. Their relationship with her was more relaxed – she even sang backup on some of their songs, including **Weeping Eyes** here – and the trio made three albums that were licensed to Virgin Records' Front Line subsidiary in the UK.

At the time, Culture were commercially successful and warmly received by the critics; they toured the UK, and played the 1978 Peace Concert in Kingston, alongside Bob Marley and other top acts. In 1980, when Virgin began to withdraw from the reggae market, the group ended their fruitful association with Mrs Pottinger. Soon after cutting some tracks for the US-based label Nighthawk (released on the compilation *Calling Rastafari*), they split up. Joseph Hill went on under the name Culture, reuniting with former members of the Soul Defenders for the excellent 1982 set *Lion Rock* on Sonic Sounds. In 1986, he got back with Albert and Kenneth, and the revived original lineup recorded and toured steadily until the early 1990s. Kenneth left in late 1992, Albert carried on for a while after; today Joseph continues to tour with different backing singers and a new young band, and still releases fresh material in the Culture style – 1996's *One Stone* is a worthy recent offering – that he has made his own.

Most of the songs on *Trod On* were recorded at Channel One studio with Sly Dunbar and the Revolutionaries. Despite a certain similarity in approach to Burning Spear, Joseph Hill is his own man. If anything, his songwriting is more varied than his oft-cited influence. Whether on hypnotic, chant-driven singles like **Ticklish Ghetto** (released on 45 in 1977 as "Work On Natty"), the uplifting **Trod On**, the hymnal **Weeping Eyes** and **No Sin**, or the alternative version of the huge 1977 UK hit **Fussing and Fighting**, a unique and coherent vision permeates these twelve songs. It's at its purest on the previously unreleased session that ends this CD, where Hill sings 'nyahbingi' versions of "No Sin" and "Weeping Eyes" with Count Ossie and the Mystic Revelation Of Rastafari – twelve minutes that are almost worth the price of this disc on their own.

⮞ We almost chose **Two Sevens Clash**, Shanachie, US, 1989

28

Janet-Lee Davis

Missing You

Fashion, 1994, UK

Recorded 1994. Janet-Lee Davis (vocals). Musicians include Sly Dunbar (drums), Clevie Browne (drums), Steely Johnson (bass, kbds), Leroy Davies (kbds), Leroy 'Mafia' Heywood (bass, drms, kbds). Produced by Chris Lane and Gussy P.

Despite so often being dismissed by lovers of hard roots music as lightweight and ephemeral, there's no denying the continuing appeal of UK lovers rock – at least among its target audience in Britain's inner cities. The original tunes that rocked 'blues parties' in the mid to late 1970s continue to be 'revive session' favourites, while the last two decades have seen an increasing sophistication in the music.

At the forefront of the 1980s advances in both production and performance values were two South London record labels: the Mad Professor's Ariwa in Thornton Heath, and Chris Lane and John MacGillivray's Fashion in Forest Hill. Fashion made its initial impact in 1980 with a classic of the genre, Dee Sharp's immaculate cut of Leo Hall's Jamaican hit of 1975 "Let's Dub It Up". After that they covered virtually every aspect of contemporary reggae, but returned repeatedly to lovers rock, with particularly worthwhile results from talents such as Winsome, Nerious Joseph, Michael Gordon and Barry Boom.

Janet-Lee Davis, who was born in 1963 in South London, was another fine singer whose considerable vocal gifts unfolded with her work for Fashion in the 1990s. She made a strong impression at the start of the decade with her 'combination' effort with Jamaican deejay Papa San, "You Love Me", which employed the

A-Class Crew's take on the Pocomania rhythms then in fashion, and with her cut of "Saving Forever", in 1993, over a version of the Studio One classic that gave the label its name, "Hi Fashion Dub".

Neither tune is included on the stunning **Missing You** set, arguably the best on the label, but it does boast two of Janet's most popular sides: a beautiful version of the Independents' US soul smash from the early 1970s, **Baby I've Been Missing You** (plus a remix with one of the Saxon sound's original chatters, Tippa Irie), and the yearningly soulful **Do You Remember**. Another highlight, **We Can Work It Out**, was released as a single after the album had appeared, and should have been a much bigger hit – her marvellous duet with the UK's top male reggae singer, the inimitable Peter Hunnigale. As it is, the song, which employed a sample from Louisa Marks' lovers classic "Six Sixth Street", will no doubt continue to be requested at 'revive' sessions long after better-selling contemporaries are forgotten.

A common barb cast in the direction of lovers rock is the form's reliance on US soul hits for material. There can be few finer comebacks to such criticism than the exquisite versions here of the Miracles' 1964 hit **Ooh Baby Baby** and Barbara Mason's 1965 soft soul smash **Yes I'm Ready**. As well as showing great taste, both tracks are ideal vehicles for Davis's own emotive intonations and interpretive power – qualities sometimes overlooked by those always seeking the radically new. Just to demonstrate Davis's prowess with fresh material, we also get **Girl On the Side**, **Your Sweet Love**, **Big Mistake**, and **Who's That Girl** – songs that beautifully express the different feelings of love with a mature, realistic edge.

The feel of a quality production is confirmed by the list of musicians involved, which includes Kingston's top drum and bass partnership, Sly Dunbar and Robbie Shakespeare, plus their London counterparts, Mafia and Fluxy. Sly and Robbie associate Lloyd 'Gitsy' Willis and producer Chris Lane both add tasteful guitar, while Tim Saunders contributes some fine tenor sax.

⮑ We almost chose **Various – Lovers Fashion Vol. 1**, Fashion, 1996

29

Desmond Dekker and the Aces

The Original Reggae Hit Sound

Trojan, 1988, UK

Recorded 1965–70. Desmond Dekker (vocals). Musicians include Hux Brown (gtr), Gladstone Anderson (pno), Ansel Collins (organ), Paul Douglas (drums), Lynn Taitt (gtr), Lloyd Parks (bass), Winston Wright (organ). Produced by Leslie Kong.

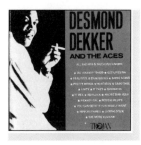

Before Bob Marley became his country's one global superstar, the former welder Desmond Dekker – born in Kingston in 1942 as Desmond Dacres – enjoyed greater international success than any other Jamaican performer. When he auditioned for Clement Dodd and Duke Reid in the early 1960s, however, he was rejected by both. His first break came when he teamed up with Wilson James and Easton Barrington Howard, and recorded their debut single as Desmond Dekker and the Aces, "Honour Your Mother and Father", for Leslie Kong's Beverley's label. An accomplished generic ska effort, it did well enough in the Jamaican charts in 1963 to be released on Chris Blackwell's Island label in the UK. 1964's "Jeserine" was also a sizeable Jamaican hit, and appeared on the same British imprint, but the group had to wait a couple of years before they struck as strong a chord with Jamaican record buyers again.

At the end of 1966, Jamaican music was going through one of its periodic rebirths, as the hectic pace of ska slowed down and a new refinement and coolness became apparent. The way was being paved for the emergence of rock steady by tunes that celebrated the rudeboys – the young delinquents of the West Kingston ghettoes. In keeping with the rudies' love of lawless movie imagery, Desmond Dekker and the Aces' 007 **(Shanty**

Town) employed memorable references to both James Bond and *Ocean's 11*. In 1967, it hit the number 14 slot in the UK, and – somewhat more surprisingly – also charted in the US.

That song opens **The Original Hit Sound**, the most comprehensive collection of Dekker's hits currently available. This nineteen-track set misses most of the Aces' ska material, apart from the glorious **Get Up Edina** and **Wise Man**, and the less successful rudie follow-ups to their first international smash, "Rude Boy Train" and "Rudie Got Soul". The Jamaican hit of 1967, "Mother Young Gal", and 1968's Festival Song winner, "Intensified", are also omitted. However, it does include most of their local hits, and everything that made the UK charts. The year after "007 (Shanty Town)" reached far beyond the Jamaican emigre community in the UK, the Jamaican hit "A It Mek" was remixed for the world market. As **It Mek**, it climbed to number seven in the UK charts. "Poor Mi Israelites" benefited from another remix in a London studio to become Dekker's biggest international seller of all. Again, there was some retitling, and as **Israelites** it topped the UK charts in April 1969, enjoyed similar success in West Germany, Sweden, Holland, Canada and South Africa, and even reached the top ten in the US.

One way in which Dekker's hit-making career differed from that of most Jamaican performers was in his loyalty to just one producer – the Chinese-Jamaican who had given him his start. Whether out of appreciation of Leslie Kong's very professional approach in the studio, or his reliability with regards to royalty cheques, every Dekker record until the producer's premature death in 1971 appeared on the Beverley's label.

Despite what's missing, this CD makes a superb introduction to Kong's clean, commercial sound, as well as the distinctive tenor of a talent too often taken for granted – just check lesser-known tracks such as **Beautiful and Dangerous**, **Sabotage**, and **Pretty Africa** – or **Unity**, which was only beaten in the Jamaican Festival Song Contest of 1967 by the Jamaicans' Treasure Isle classic "Ba Ba Boom Time".

⮑ We almost chose **Writing On The Wall**, Trojan, UK, 1998

30

Coxsone Dodd/Various Artists

Respect To Studio One

Heartbeat, 1994, US/UK

Recorded 1965–80. Produced by Coxsone Dodd. Artists include the Heptones, Marcia Griffiths, Slim Smith, Larry Marshall, Burning Spear, Horace Andy, Sugar Minott, Alton Ellis, Ken Boothe, Lee Perry, Freddie McGregor, Johnnie Osbourne, the Skatalites, the Wailers, Jackie Mittoo, Don Drummond, Roland Alphonso.

Studio One is often characterized as the Jamaican Motown – owner Clement 'Coxsone' Dodd even used the slogan "The Sound Of Young Jamaica" on his Jamaican radio show and record sleeves – but the analogy is not quite exact. Studio One has been central to the development of Jamaican music in a way that the Detroit counterpart never was to the evolution of soul. Like Berry Gordy at Motown, Coxsone actively sought out and trained new talent, holding auditions at the studio he opened on Brentford Road in 1962, which became a musical college for singers, deejays, and musicians. The two-CD **Respect to Studio One** set, compiled as a sampler for Heartbeat's reissue programme, serves as a wonderful miniature history of Jamaican music, portrayed through recordings – classic ska, rock steady and dancehall – from its most influential label.

The set kicks off with a clip from the label's radio show in 1970, with disc jockey Winston Williams in alliterative full flight. The first selection, the Heptones' **Pretty Looks Isn't All**, epitomizes Studio One at its best. A bittersweet masterpiece, its rhythm has been repeatedly recut ever since 1968. Nearly all the tracks could be commented on in similar terms, like Larry Marshall's pivotal **Nanny Goat**, one of the first records to use the reggae rhythm, or Carlton and the Shoes' **Love Me**

Forever, a perfect harmony vocal wedded to an irrepressible bass line. Slim Smith's **Never Let Go** too has inspired hundreds of recuts, while Burning Spear's **Fire Down Below**, from 1969, prefigures his later roots classics.

Most of Jamaica's best singers get a look in. The first CD – all boss reggae and sweet rock steady, mostly from 1968 to 1970 – has Delroy Wilson, Marcia Griffiths, Horace Andy, Ken Boothe, John Holt, and 1970s dancehall originator Sugar Minott, whose **Vanity** (from 1975) uses Alton Ellis' "I'm Just A Guy" rhythm (from 1967). Coxsone was among the first to realize the potential for originating further versions by re-using old rhythms – studio engineer Sylvan Morris and assistant Larry Marshall cut thousands of dubplates for sound systems between 1968 and 1972. Coxsone dubs – like the Brentford All Stars' **Throw Me Corn** here – are heard in the dancehall to this day. Without the music created at Studio One during the 1960s and 1970s, reggae would just not exist on the scale it does today, nor in the forms it uses. Since the early 1980s, songs using recut rhythms have accounted for up to fifty percent of 'new' releases.

The second CD includes several late-1970s songs that used 1960s rhythms, like Freddy McGregor's **Bobby Bobylon**, and Willie Williams' **Armagideon Time** (covered by the Clash). Finally, there are six superb ska tracks, with the great instrumental band the Skatalites covering the Beatles, the Wailers' 1963 rudeboy anthem **Simmer Down**, and Ken Boothe and Stranger Cole's fevered **Artibella** absolutely outstanding among them.

Ultimately, this 32-track set is a tribute to the taste of Clement Seymour Dodd, without whose approval nothing was recorded at Studio One. Although he never wrote a note or a word of lyric, his early years as a fan of US styles like bebop and r'n'b stood him in great stead when listening to the flood of new talent. His selecting ability informs everything here; it's as good an introduction to reggae's premier studio as you'll find, and convincing proof of Studio One's innovation, quality and influence.

⮡ We almost chose **Best of Studio One Vol.1**, Heartbeat, USA/UK 1987

31

Coxsone Dodd and Duke Reid

Sir Coxsone and Duke Reid In Concert At Forresters' Hall

Studio One, 1995, US

Recorded 1959–63. Various artists. Produced by Coxsone Dodd and Duke Reid.

In its earliest incarnation, from the late 1940s and on through the 1950s, the sound system – a mobile discotheque, with massive bass-heavy speakers – was a uniquely Jamaican institution. Legendary sounds such as Count Nick the Champ, Goodies, and Tom the Great Sebastian were followed by those who were eventually to produce their own music – King Edwards, Sir Coxsone Downbeat, and Duke Reid the Trojan. Their music was the hard-edged US r'n'b of performers like Amos Milburn, Willis Jackson and Wynonie Harris.

By the late 1950s, however, the supply of the kind of US boogie and shuffle records popular with Jamaica dancers had dried up. The owners of several leading sounds started to record local musicians, initially hoping to emulate US models. Arch-rivals Clement 'Sir Coxsone' Dodd and Arthur 'Duke' Reid, two of the biggest names in the dancehall, both played major roles in the island's fledgling recording business, developing a music that took on a distinctly Jamaican feel under the name of ska. Later still, the Duke was to record beautiful music that was the essence of rock steady, and eventually launch the deejay phenomenon with ground-breaking hits by U-Roy, while the Sir was responsible for outstanding music in every era, as well as being the first producer regularly to re-press his old hits.

Despite their intense rivalry, the Duke and the Sir never played opposite each other in one of Jamaica's legendary 'clashes', which involved attempting to 'flop' a rival in the dance with the hottest and most exclusive tunes. Instead, they were content to try and draw customers away from each other's dances with the promise of their set's sound quality, selections and deejays (who had already started delivering jivetalk over the records).

Dodd's 1995 release of **In Concert at Forresters' Hall** was an attempt to recreate what such a clash would have been like had it taken place, featuring four of the Duke's hits and a more generous selection of Coxsone's own. The date of this clash would have had to be in the early 1960s as, along with the shuffles of the previous decade, a couple of early ska tunes are included. The Skatalites, who officially formed in 1964, are represented by one of the many TV- or movie-inspired ska tunes, **Twilight Zone**. Recorded for Reid, it sounds as strong as their better-known Studio One hits "Dr. Kildare", "James Bond" and "Dick Tracy". Then there's a classic example of vocal ska that's also fittingly an early 'sound war' tune: one of the adolescent Delroy Wilson's series of hits for Coxsone, aimed at the ascendant Prince Buster, **Duke & the Sir** (aka "Spit In the Sky").

Like the majority of tunes here, **What Makes Honey** belongs to the shuffle-boogie mould that kickstarted the Jamaican recording business. It should not, incidentally, be credited to the Skatalites, but, as it was on one of the first Blue Beat releases in the UK, to Duke Reid's Group. Three other instrumentals pay tribute to key musical locations. For Coxsone, Clue J and the Blues Blasters – featuring both trumpeter Johnny 'Dizzy' Moore and trombonist Rico Rodriguez in brilliant form – offer **Milk Lane Hop** and **Five Minutes On Beeston Street**, while Duke's Group has **Pink Lane Hop**. In truth, there was not a great deal to distinguish the two producers' styles at the time when most of these tracks were recorded – neither had their own studio yet – and the real winner in the 'clash' has to be anyone with the slightest interest in the roots of reggae.

⮑ We almost chose **It's Shuffle & Skatime**, Jamaica/Gold, Holland, 1994

32

The Dynamites

Are The Wild Reggae Bunch

Jamaican Gold, 1996, Netherlands

Musicians include Hux Brown (gtr), Clifton 'Jackie' Jackson (bass), Paul Douglas (drums), Gladstone Anderson (piano), Winston 'Brubeck' Wright (organ). Produced by Clancy Eccles.

Session musicians are the true heroes of reggae. The players on **The Dynamites Are The Wild Reggae Bunch** recorded under a variety of names for Clancy Eccles, Duke Reid, Derrick Harriott and Leslie Kong in the late 1960s and 1970s, supplying rhythm for numerous hits. When we talk about 'rock steady' or 'reggae', we are talking about styles they created, with others similarly unsung.

Producer Clancy Eccles gave the group the name Dynamites because they "sounded like something was going to explode". The key players – noted above – made around two hundred sides with Eccles. The basic band was often augmented in the studio by such luminaries as Ernest Ranglin (guitar), Aubrey Adams (organ) and Val Bennett (sax), among others. The organist Winston 'Brubeck' Wright was one of the most unsung players in reggae history. In addition to Dynamite duties, he wrote "The Liquidator" – a massive hit for producer Harry Johnson (to whom he sold it outright). He died in 1992, in penurious circumstances following a heart attack. Similarly, Val Bennett, who had a UK Top 10 chart hit with The Upsetters' "Return of Django", died in a Kingston almshouse in 1991, his legs amputated.

The programme on *The Dynamites Are The Wild Reggae*

Bunch combines reggae versions of well-known (and often distinctly unpromising) material with tunes written by producer Clancy Eccles, who would hum his melodies to the musicians. Among non-original tracks, there are easy-listening takes on such as Allan Sherman's **Hello Muddah**, the Beatles' **Hey Jude** and Neil Diamond's "Holly Holy" (**I Fe Layo**). Two tunes are based on South African songs - **Mr Midnight** is a version of "Skoiaan" while **The Lion Wakes** adapts the Zulu song "Wimoweh" (which had been a hit for US vocal group The Tokens in 1961 as "The Lion Sleeps Tonight").

Wright's distinctive organ is the lead instrument on many of the most popular cuts. His sound is characterized by the wide vibrato and bell-like voicings he extracts from the keyboard, as on the version of the US r'n'b oldie **Riding West**, a Jamaican dancehall favourite when originally recorded by drummer Billy Hope in 1958. But most of the musicians get to solo, ensuring variety. Val Bennett contributes virile tenor sax to **Mercilina** and **City Demonstration**; Charlie 'Organaire' Cameron's plaintive harmonica enlivens the smooth rock steady of **Western Organ**; and Carl Masters delivers effectively blustering trombone to **The Struggle**. Hux Brown's distinctively picked rhythm guitar is a delight throughout, as is the rock solid Jackie Jackson.

In the 1970s, several of these influential musicians went on to back Toots & the Maytals, then heading for international success. Clancy Eccles himself, a lifelong socialist, became politically active in the late Michael Manley's People's National Party playing an important role in their successful 1972 election campaign. He virtually retired from music by the end of the decade and his catalogue has often been overlooked. However, this wonderful set (and other Eccles compilations in Jamaican Gold's excellent series of early reggae reissues) should go some way to re-establishing his reputation.

➲ Almost chose **Lloyd Chalmers: Psychedelic Reggae**, Tribute, UK, 1999

33

Alton Ellis

Cry Tough

Heartbeat, 1993, US

Recorded 1966–68. Alton Ellis (vocals). Produced by Arthur 'Duke' Reid.

Calling to mind such fruitful producer–artist relationships as Elvis and Sam Phillips, Al Green and Willie Mitchell, or Bob Marley and Lee Perry, the music that Alton Ellis made for Arthur 'Duke' Reid (1915–1976) scaled heights that the singer has since equalled but never bettered. Born in Kingston in 1944, Alton Ellis started his recording career with Coxsone Dodd. He was half of the duo Alton and Eddy (Perkins), who came to prominence on the Vere Johns talent shows then held in Kingston cinemas. They cut the moving prison ballad "Muriel", which became a big hit, at Dodd's first commercial session in 1959.

In the years that followed, Alton worked again for Dodd, as well as for Vincent Chin of Randy's Records, and he also began recording for Duke Reid, cutting a version of Chris Kenner's New Orleans r'n'b hit "Something You Got" in 1964. He wasn't Reid's number one singer in the ska days; that honour went first to Stranger Cole, and later to Justin Hinds. But Duke loved the way Alton sang, commenting one day that "Boy, it a sound like you a cry"; Alton replied, "No Duke, is not cry, is SOUL . . ."

In 1966, Ellis recorded **Girl I've Got A Date**, and everything changed. As rock steady swept away the last of ska, Duke Reid became the leading producer on the island, and Alton Ellis became one of its leading voices. Many singers subsequently mimicked his phrasing, including the young Dennis Brown, while Alton's vocal persona of the lonely anguished lover would be adopted by such as Gregory Isaacs.

The **Cry Tough** compilation is a delight from start to finish. As well as most of Alton's Treasure Isle album *Mr Soul Of Jamaica*, it includes eight extra tracks, four of them otherwise unreleased. Of these latter four, two are soul versions of familiar songs, including "Girl I've Got A Date", and the resolutely anti-macho **I'm Just A Guy**, originally done in a rock steady version for Dodd at Studio One, but here recast as a soul duet with Phyllis Dillon. There are also several covers of US soul hits – Chuck Jackson's **Willow Tree** is perhaps even better than the original, while Junior Walker's **What Does It Take**, Johnnie Taylor's **Ain't That Loving You**, the Delfonics' **La La Means I Love You**, and Blood Sweat and Tears' **You Made Me So Very Happy** at least equal the versions that inspired them.

The originals here are no less brilliant. Check how Alton's voice soars over the backing chorus on **Why Birds Follow Spring**, or the understated lyricism of **If I Could Rule This World** – no one had ever sung like that in Jamaica before him. Other highlights include the socially aware masterpiece **Black Man, White Man** (aka "Black Man's Pride"), the anti-badman **Cry Tough**, directed to the notorious mid-1960s gunman Busby, and the discomix length **Can't Stand It**. This latter tune is the version reissued in 1977 by Sonia Pottinger, with witty U-Roy imitator Ranking Trevor adding the deejay toast. Several songs are issued in slightly variant, previously unreleased takes that, amazingly, are as good as the better-known cuts.

The crisp remastering enhances the superb musicianship of the Treasure Isle session band, Tommy McCook and the Supersonics. The leader played tenor sax and flute, with Herman Marquis on alto sax, Winston Wright on organ, Lynn Taitt and Ernest Ranglin on guitars, Jackie Jackson on bass, and Hugh Malcolm on drum. When matched with one of the style's greatest singers, the results are unbeatable: as Alton himself said years later: "I sing like a bird – man, I couldn't stop."

➲ We almost chose **Sunday Coming**, Studio One, US, 1995

34

The Ethiopians

The Original Reggae Hit Sound of the Ethiopians

Trojan, 1986, UK

Recorded 1966–72. The Ethiopians: Leonard Dillon (vocals), Stephen Taylor (vocals), Aston Morris (vocals). Producers include Coxsone Dodd, Sonia Pottinger, J.J. Johnson, Derrick Harriott, Duke Reid.

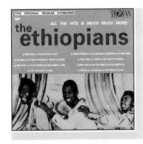

One of the most consistent Jamaican vocal groups ever, and the first to sport an overtly Rastafarian name, the Ethiopians were formed when Leonard Dillon, who had made a couple of records under the name of Jack Sparrow in 1965, linked up with Stephen Davis and Aston Morris. Working initially for Clement Dodd, they notched up late ska/early rock steady hits in 1966 and 1967 such as "Free Man", "I'm Gonna Take Over Now" and "Live Good". In addition to Dillon's distinctive tenor, their music stood out as almost invariably expressing the ghetto sufferer's perspective, as opposed to the rudeboy braggadocio then fashionable. After Morris left the group, the Ethiopians continued as a duo, recording major hits for WIRL and Sonia Pottinger.

As the music shifted yet again, to become reggae, they joined 'Sir' J.J. Johnson, with whom they recorded at least twenty sides. In the UK, Trojan released the Johnson-produced *Reggae Power* album, a more consistent set than their first, the now very collectible *Engine 54* for WIRL. At the end of the 1960s, the duo freelanced for different bosses, including Derrick Harriott, Alvin Ranglin, Lee Perry, H. Robinson, Lloyd Daley, Harry Johnson, Duke Reid, Rupie Edwards and Winston Riley. A car crash killed Stephen Taylor in 1975, but Dillon carried on. The *Slave Call* and *Open the Gate Of Zion* albums, for Niney and Alvin Ranglin respectively, appeared in the late 1970s, followed by *Everything Crash* on Studio One, a masterpiece of reflective cultural material that was credited to 'the Ethiopian'. Too little has been heard of Leonard Dillon since then.

While the sheer number of producers for whom the Ethiopians worked makes a definitive compilation almost impossible, the **Original Hit Sound** anthology comes as close as possible on a single disc. Its 21 tracks begin with **Free Man**, from Studio One, which pretty much defined the Ethiopians' enduring approach, regardless of their producer, or even the singers behind Dillon. That's the only example of their Brentford Road output here, but it's followed by four equally essential tracks for WIRL. **Train To Skaville** sold particularly well in the UK, though it's somewhat atypical in being effectively an instrumental, in which the group's role is restricted to the train's whistle, the chorus and spoken interjections. Trains were a popular topic of the day, and they also cut **Engine 54** for WIRL and **Train To Glory** for Sonia Pottinger. Even more successful for Pottinger was **The Whip**, another semi-instrumental; like "Train to Skaville", it has been repeatedly 'versioned' ever since, with new cuts rocking dancehalls even today.

The group's most consistent run of all was with J.J. Johnson, eleven of whose productions are included here. **Everything Crash** dealt with the considerable social unrest in Jamaica, including strikes in several public utilities. Like **Hong Kong Flu**, it features a cracking example of the confident new reggae beat. Slower tunes like **Things A Get Bad To Worse**, **One**, and **The Selah**, on the other hand, looked to the future, with the last two based on the sort of traditional Rasta chants that Dillon was to employ on the *Slave Call* album. The remaining tracks from Derrick Harriott, Duke Reid and Harry Johnson are of a similar calibre, and further confirm the crucial – if undersung – role of the Ethiopians in the development of reggae.

⮞ We almost chose **Owner Fi De Yard**, Heartbeat, US/UK, 1996

35

Marcia Griffiths

Indomitable

Penthouse, 1992, US/UK

Recorded 1993. Musicians include Steely & Clevie and Mafia & Fluxy (bass, kbds, drums), Tony Rebel, Cutty Ranks and Buju Banton (deejay vocals). Produced by Donovan Germain.

Indomitable is an apt title for this CD. Marcia Griffiths (born 1950, Kingston) has been Jamaica's leading female vocalist for well over thirty years, and its most consistent interpreter of quality songs ever since Philip James of soul duo the Blues Busters introduced her to Byron Lee. When the 15-year old Marcia appeared at a Dragonaires stage show on Easter Monday 1965 she brought the house down.

Following the gig, the teenager was signed up by Clement Dodd, though he had to wait until 1968 for her first hit – the joyous **Feel Like Jumping**. At Studio One, Marcia became linked with Bob Andy, recording several of his compositions (including "Melody Life", "Truly" and "Mark My Words"); they later recorded as a duo for Harry Johnson, scoring in the UK charts in 1970–71 with pop-reggae covers of Nina Simone's "Young Gifted & Black" and Crispian St Peters' "Pied Piper".

In 1975, Marcia became a member of Bob Marley's I-Threes – with Rita Marley and Judy Mowatt touring with the superstar until his death in 1981. She found time to record two superb albums for Sonia Pottinger (*Naturally* and *Steppin'*) in the late 1970s, and cut tracks for Bunny Wailer in the same period. She recorded "Electric Boogie" for the ex-Wailer in 1981 – and eight years later it was a surprise US pop hit.

Shortly after that success, Marcia joined forces with Donovan Germain. This astute producer began issuing records by the Diamonds and others in the '70s, gained crossover hits in the UK with Sugar Minott and Freddie McGregor in the first half of the 1980s, and became increasingly successful as the decade ended. If King Jammy is the Coxsone Dodd of the digital period then Germain is surely its Duke Reid. He opened Penthouse Studio in 1987 and with his right hand man Dave 'Rude Boy' Kelly created hits for many artists, not only in the dominant deejay style. Jamaica's leading soul singer Beres Hammond became a star when working at the studio; Marcia soon followed, her voice sounding better than ever over the modern Penthouse rhythms. These were laid by all the leading teams – Steely & Clevie, Sly & Robbie, Firehouse Crew and Danny Browne.

Indomitable was Marcia's second album for Penthouse, recorded between 1991 and 93, and captures her in excellent voice. It kicks off with **Fire Burning**, Germain's inspired blend of two Bob Andy songs cleverly welding the original melody and lyric to the rhythm of Andy's "Feeling Soul". The deejay version with Cutty Ranks was an even bigger hit as a 12-inch and he appears on three other combinations here – **Loving You**, **My Lover** and **Check It Out** – the latter in company with the label's other deejay stars, Tony Rebel and Buju Banton. Marcia also confidently revisits **Feel Like Jumping**, her first Studio One hit; riding Germain's sample-laden new cut, only the bass line from the original is retained. Beres Hammond's **Closer To You** used the studio's successful revival of the "Nanny Goat" rhythm, hot in the 1992 dancehall.

But it's her interpretative gifts that hold the attention here. Beautifully voiced and overflowing with warmth, the buoyant recuts of John Holt's **My Satisfaction**, Delano Stewart's **That's Life** and Johnnie Osbourne's **Warrior** are outstanding. A truly uplifting take of Miriam Makeba's **I Shall Sing** confirms her supremacy; it could also be her professional credo.

➲ We almost chose **Truly**, Heartbeat, US/UK, 1998

36

Beres Hammond

A Love Affair

Penthouse, 1992, UK

Recorded 1991–92. Beres Hammond (vocals). Musicians include Steely & Clevie and Mafia & Fluxy (bass, kbds, drums). Produced by Donovan Germain.

As implied by the title of his 1979 debut album, *Soul Reggae*, Beres Hammond was for many years Jamaica's foremost soul stylist. Occupying a comfortable niche in the island's music scene, he remained far removed from the latest dancehall trends. Born Beresford Hammond in Kingston in 1955, and blessed with a warm, rich voice, his career began in the mid-1970s with the highly rated Zap Pow band. His is the voice on their hit, "This Is Reggae Music", and he also cut the now ultra-rare "revive" favourite, "Why ?", for Harold Butler.

Records such as "One Step Ahead" in 1978, "I'm in Love With You" in 1979, and "If Only I Knew" in 1981 registered strongly with Jamaican record buyers, but the next four years saw no further hits. In 1985, the Willie Lindo-produced "One Dance Will Do", a version of Prince Buster's "Shaking Up Orange Street" rhythm, gave Hammond a taste of real dancehall popularity. Audrey Hall's response, "One Dance Won't Do", was an unexpected UK pop hit, but the original never carried beyond the reggae market. In the same year, "Groovy Little Thing" was another major Jamaican hit. Then, once again, Hammond's output resumed its failure to sell in the deserved quantities. Until he linked up with producer Donovan Germain at the start of the 1990s, he seemed destined to remain on Jamaica's North Coast hotel circuit.

Germain, a former New York resident, had opened his Penthouse studio in Kingston in 1987, and was making some of the most accomplished digital reggae since King Jammy's pioneering hits with computerized rhythms. He hit upon the notion of taking the adult tones of Beres Hammond – who was very much a singer in the traditional sense – and placing them over the latest dancehall rhythms. Their initial success together came with **Tempted To Touch**, a typical Hammond tale of his love not being returned, delivered over a crisp updating of John Holt's "A Love I Can Feel" rhythm. Germain followed this sublime shot with a string of further hits in a similar mould, which he collected on the album **A Love Affair** a year later. Its success completely validated his move to juxtapose Hammond over modern dancehall rhythms, and established the singer as the major Jamaican vocalist of the digital age.

The singles – including "Tempted To Touch", **Feeling Lonely**, **After the Fight**, **Is This A Sign**, and **Falling In Love Again** – still sound as soulfully convincing as when they were rocking dancehalls and climbing the reggae charts. Rather than hurriedly adding a few fillers to the hits, however, Germain obviously lavished considerable time and attention over each of the other tracks as well. Talented musicians such as Steely and Clevie, North London's Mafia and Fluxy, the Firehouse Crew, the saxophonist Dean Frazer, and Clevie's brothers, Dalton and Danny Browne, provided the melodic rhythms. Then the cream of the island's singers make guest appearances. Marcia Griffiths, Freddie McGregor, Dennis Brown, and Glen Ricks all join Beres for the beautiful semi-acoustic **Love Within the Music**, while Marcia can also be heard on the equally strong **Live On**.

The CD release adds five extra tracks to the vinyl LP. Top Penthouse deejays Cutty Ranks, Cobra and Tony Rebel have their say on, respectively, "Tempted To Touch", "Feeling Lonely" and **Respect**. All are in majestic form, and the Cutty Ranks track proved to be a major hit in its own right.

⊃ We almost chose **Collector's Series**, Germain, US, 1998

37

The Heptones

Sea Of Love

Heartbeat, 1993, US

Recorded 1967–69. The Heptones (vocals). Musicians include Jackie Mittoo (kbds), Leroy 'Horsemouth' Wallace, Bunny Williams and Phil Callender (drums), Leroy Sibbles and Bryan Atkinson (bass), Roland Alphonso (tenor sax), Headley Bennett (alto sax). Produced by Coxsone Dodd.

Along with the Techniques, the Paragons, Gaylads and Melodians, the Heptones are the epitome of classic Jamaican group singing. They pretty much ran dancehall in the late 1960s and set the standards that all others sought to emulate. **Sea Of Love**, a superbly well-assembled CD, happily captures a significant part of that process.

The trio – Leroy Sibbles (born 1949), Earl Morgan (born 1945) and Barry Llewellyn (born 1947) – were all Kingston-born and grew up together in Trenchtown. They recorded their debut single – "Gunmen Coming To Town" – in 1964 for Syrian-Jamaican producer B.J. 'Bobby' Calnek's Caltone label, initially calling themselves The Sylastians. Then Earl found a cough mixture bottle bearing the legend 'Heptones Tonic' and the group name was settled.

In 1966, the Heptones auditioned for Studio One, where their hits began almost immediately, with such songs as "Fatty Fatty", "Baby" and "Why Did You Leave?" Over the next few years they became the leading vocal group at Studio One, recording five albums and dozens of singles for the label. Sibbles, one of reggae's most creative personalities, also found time to master the bass, learning on the job in a jazz trio led by master keyboard player Jackie Mittoo. He went on to contribute bass lines to some of the most enduring Studio One rhythms of all time: the

Abyssinians' "Satta" and "Declaration Of Rights", Carlton & the Shoes' "Love Me Forever", and the Sound Dimension's "Full Up".

Virtually anything the Heptones did at Studio One is essential. We chose *Sea Of Love* over *On Top* (see below), because for sound quality (crisp remasterings of sixteen cuts from the Coxsone vaults) and presentation it wins hands down; nonetheless, having heard this disc you'll want the other, for songs like "Pretty Looks", "I Hold The Handle", "Equal Rights" and "Party Time". Not that *Sea of Love* lacks its share of classics. These include late 1960s dancehall hits like **Get In The Groove**, **Be A Man** and **Love Won't Come Easy** as well as **Sea Of Love** itself – Phil Phillips' swamp-pop chestnut.

Although Leroy Sibbles is usually regarded as the key singer and writer in the group, the other Heptones are no makeweights. Barry Llewellyn, an accomplished writer and lead vocalist in his own right, sings lead on four tracks here, most impressively so on **Nine Pound Steel** and **Stick Man**. Earl Morgan is the harmony man par excellence, and a contributing writer too, and on **Please Be True**, Anthony 'Rocky' Ellis sings lead, with the trio supplying their trademark harmonies.

Sibbles' perfect tenor – achingly fragile or huskily entreating by turn – graces the remaining songs, as subtly persuasive on beautiful originals like **Ting A Ling** or **Love Me With All Of Your Heart** as on the cover versions – Weldon Irving and Nina Simone's **Young Gifted and Black** and Cynthia Weil, Barry Mann and Phil Spector's **You've Lost That Loving Feeling**. The immediate warmth of his vocals is apparent even when singing lead in close harmony with Barry and Earl – as here, on the covers of Curtis Mayfield's **Choice Of Colours** or Bob Dylan's **I Shall Be Released**.

Although the trio split up after successful albums for Lee Perry and others in the 1970s, they reformed in the 1990s to become a much-loved feature of revival shows. They have also been in the studio together recently, for producer Niney and others.

➲ We almost chose **On Top**, Studio One, US, 1997

38

John Holt

Time Is The Master

Moodisc, 1993, US

Recorded 1971–73. John Holt (vocals), Gladstone Anderson (kbds). Produced by Harry A. Mudie.

John Holt first came to fame during the rock steady era, as the lead singer of the immortal Paragons. By the time he made **Time Is The Master** for Spanish Town producer Harry A. Mudie, he had gone on to enjoy an equally successful solo career, with Duke Reid, Coxsone Dodd and Bunny Lee. The formula here – velvet-smooth vocals imparting "quality" love songs, surrounded by lush string and horn arrangements – would be used by Holt and producer Tony Ashfield for a series of albums on Trojan Records in the mid-'70s. Those sets – *The Further You Look* and *1000 Volts Of Holt*, with their striking Ras Dan Heartman cover paintings, and the anodyne *2000 Volts* follow-up – sold massively in the UK. Holt's rendition of Kris Kristofferson's "Help Me Make It Through The Night" stayed high in the UK charts for three months from December 1974.

However, *Time Is The Master* is preferable to the Trojan albums; the strength of the rhythms, and their prominence in the mix, helps to avoid the "background music" effect so prevalent on the later albums. In addition, Holt himself sounds more engaged with the material; the songs are well chosen, and coincidentally shed light on the influence in Jamaica of US r'n'b and country music. Vocalists such as Nat King Cole and Brook Benton were enormously popular on the island, with fans including singers like the late Wilfred 'Jackie' Edwards. John covers two songs associated with Nat King Cole here, **Again** and the brilliant **Looking Back**, written by Brook Benton and Clyde Otis for Cole in 1958. Aided immeasurably by the warmth of his delivery and a beautiful arrangement, Holt imbues the latter, wherein a man reviews his life and his mistakes with regret, with just the right degree of sincerity. Mudie has also voiced Gregory Isaacs on the rhythm, but this version is the essential one. Holt gives similarly definitive readings to Ivory Joe Hunter's country-tinged r'n'b ballad **It May Sound Silly**, the Tams' **Riding For A Fall**, and three originals credited to producer Mudie, the reflective **Time Is The Master** and two songs of lost love – **Everybody Knows** and **Love Is Gone** – which are convincingly anguished rather than self-pitying.

Also included is **Stick By Me**, a song later made famous by UB40, who covered it on *Labour Of Love*. Originally produced by Bunny Lee, who also voiced Delroy Wilson and Dennis Brown on the song, it's a cover of a 1963 original by the US group Shep and the Limelites. Lee gave it to Mudie (with "Riding For A Fall"), who added the strings and scored with the song again. Although the very idea of strings – recorded in London by John Bell – may be anathema to roots fans, they're very sympathetic and never overdone. Contrasting against the heavy rhythm, they give a perfect setting to Holt's voice.

Holt went on to further success in the 1970s, scoring hits in the 'rockers' style with "Up Park Camp" among others. He came to the fore again in the early 1980s with producer 'Junjo' Lawes – "Police In Helicopter" and "Fat She Fat" were big dancehall hits – and has continued recording and performing ever since. This pivotal album projects his voice through songs that acknowledge his roots as a singer, in 1950s r'n'b and ballads and 1960s soul. Producer Mudie filters that material through the rhythms of early 1970s dancehall, like the John Crow skank and the one-drop. The resultant blend is then sweetened with strings, to create a sublime Jamaican version of easy-listening, like condensed milk and white rum punch.

⮑ We almost chose **A Love I Can Feel**, Studio One, US, 1997

39

Keith Hudson

Pick A Dub

Atra, 1974, UK; Blood & Fire, 1994, UK

Recorded 1973–74. Keith Hudson (producer). Musicians include the Soul Syndicate session band, plus Aston 'Family Man' Barrett (bass), Carlton Barrett (drums), Augustus Pablo (melodica), Earl 'Chinna' Smith (gtr).

The producer and singer Keith Hudson always had a pretty dismal vocal technique himself, but he certainly knew how to get the best out of others in the studio, as witnessed by the outstanding performances he gained from singers Ken Boothe, Horace Andy, Alton Ellis and John Holt. Hudson, who was born in Kingston in 1946, and died in New York in 1984, financed his early production endeavours through work as a dentist. His first major hit, Ken Boothe's "Old Fashion Way", topped the Jamaican charts in late 1967; subsequent singles included trumpeter Johnny 'Dizzy' Moore's classic instrumental "Riot". Hudson even made his own unorthodox voice an effective tool on the moody and experimental *Flesh Of My Flesh, Skin Of My Skin* album, released in the UK on Mamba in 1975.

During the early 1970s, 'versions' were all the rage, and Hudson followed his most successful vocals with outstanding deejay and instrumental cuts. Thus his initial hit "Old Fashion Way" was given classic deejay interpretations by U-Roy as "Dynamic Fashion Way" (which preceded the toaster's first hits on Treasure Isle), and Dennis Alcapone as "Spanish Omega". Deejay versions developed alongside stripped-down instrumental ones, and the progressive young producer was among the first to release an album entirely devoted to dub mixes.

Hudson's sinewy rhythm tracks, often played by the undervalued Soul Syndicate band, always seemed tailor-made for radical deconstruction. The year after the initial trickle of Jamaican dub albums appeared in 1973, **Pick A Dub** was the first to be released in the UK. Over two decades later, it's still obvious why the set immediately enjoyed healthy sales, and played such an important part in launching the ensuing mania for dub.

To begin with, Hudson chose only his hardest rhythm tracks, built by top session musicians like Aston and Carlton Barrett from the Wailers on bass and drums, Augustus Pablo on melodica, and Earl 'Chinna' Smith on guitar. To Hudson originals such as Big Youth's "S.90 Skank", the deejay's first major hit – here reworked as **Pick A Dub** – and Horace Andy's haunting **I'm All Right**, Hudson added versions of the Abyssinians' enduring "Satta Massagana" (**Satia**) and "Declaration Of Rights" (**Black Right**), both of which equalled the originals, plus an inspired cover of the Dramatics' US soul favourite, **In the Rain**. As one of the first half-dozen dub albums, *Pick A Dub* eschewed the sound effects (dogs barking, babies crying, car horns, and so on) that marked later developments. Instead what were in any case fairly sparse tracks were mixed down to their bare essentials, presumably by Hudson himself, to bring out and emphasize their original dynamics – particularly between the Barrett brothers, or the keyboards or guitar against both the drums and bass. When parts of the vocals suddenly intrude, it's always to slightly unnerving effect, with Horace Andy's echoed falsetto sounding particularly ethereal. Even Hudson's own vocal efforts sound quite compelling in such fractured forms.

In common with seminal dub sets from Lee Perry, Randy's, Prince Buster and Herman Chin Loy, Hudson's *Pick A Dub* possesses a classic simplicity. Arguably, later gimmicks and technical refinements added little to the classic form they established. Certainly there is no denying the subtlety, power and sheer spirit of adventure that distinguished this in 1974, and still make it essential to any dub selection today.

⮕ We almost chose **Brand**, Pressure Sounds, UK, 1995

40

I-Roy

Don't Check Me With No Lightweight Stuff

Blood & Fire, 1997, UK

Recorded 1972–75. I-Roy (deejay). Producers include Pete Weston, Keith Hudson, Duke Reid, Errol Thompson, Clive Choy, Bunny Lee, Jimmy Radway and I-Roy.

Of all the deejay pioneers of the 1970s, I-Roy was indubitably the most literate, and arguably the wittiest. Born Roy Samuel Reid in St Thomas, in 1944, he started his career while working as a civil servant. His reputation took off when he moved from Kingston to Spanish Town. Jamaica's former capital was home to a thriving sound system scene, and he worked on the top local sounds, moving from Son's Junior first to Rudolph 'Ruddy' Redwood's Supreme Ruler Of Sound, and then Stereo. His dancehall stature grew still further when he took the mike on the esteemed May Pen sound V-Rocket, and King Tubby's Home Town Hi Fi in West Kingston.

By the time I-Roy made his first records in 1970 for Spanish Town producer Harry Mudie, his style still bore traces of the man who had established deejaying on record earlier that year, and whose place he had sometimes taken on Tubby's sound – the great U-Roy. The influence of Dennis Alcapone was apparent as well, but much in his approach was original, and he soon developed his own unique voice: an intimate tone that had not been heard before, and a storytelling ability that few have equalled since. Four years of building his skills at the mike on sound systems had obviously paid off; when Mudie released "Musical Pleasure", followed by versions of recent hits by Dennis Walks, John Holt, and the Ebony Sisters, I-Roy quickly registered with record buyers in Jamaica and the UK, where he lived for a while deejaying with London's Sir Coxsone sound. However, it was with a move to the younger Augustus 'Gussie' Clarke, then only 19, that I-Roy's career really took off, with not only a superb series of popular 45s, but one of the most acclaimed debut deejay sets ever, the magnificent *Presenting I-Roy*.

Don't Check Me With No Lightweight Stuff covers the deejay's most prolific and successful period, starting with the one disc he made for Spanish Town sound man Ruddy Redwood – a marvellous cut of saxophonist Tommy McCook's "Sidewalk Doctor", abrasively retitled **Sidewalk Killer**. The fifteen tracks for different producers that then follow continue to pile on the musical pressure, though in the most subtle manner possible. Always the most erudite of deejays, the irrepressible I-Roy peppered his hits with references to such diverse cultural icons as thriller writer Mickey Spillane, film director Alfred Hitchcock, boxer Joe Frazier, and Black Panther Stokely Carmichael. Even Florence Nightingale and Cleopatra were name-checked.

For prime examples of his sly humour and powers of observation, check Mr Reid's tribute to the Harry Belafonte and Sydney Poitier movie **Buck and the Preacher**, and his thoughts on **Sound Education**, over Errol Dunkley's wicked "Black Cinderella". He also has plenty to add to classics like Augustus Pablo's "Java" (**Hospital Trolley**), Bob Marley's "Talking Blues" (**Straight To The Heathen's Head**), the Paragons' "Quiet Place" (**Noisy Place**), and Desmond Young's "Warning" (**Double Warning**). And then there's **Fire Burn** and **Sufferer's Psalm**, both riding the Randy's cut of the Soul Vendors' "Swing Easy", itself a rock steady interpretation of "Fiddler On the Roof".

As the man said elsewhere: "It's easier for a camel, to go through a needle's eye, than for a version to die, believe me." Listening to the I-Roy classics collected here, it's only too easy to believe – this is deejaying at its most varied, pertinent and pithy.

➲ We almost chose **Presenting.../Hell & Sorrow**, Trojan, UK, 1997

41

Gregory Isaacs

My Number One

Heartbeat, 1990, US/UK

Recorded 1976–78. Gregory Isaacs (vocals). Musicians include the GG All Stars, The Revolutionaries, Soul Syndicate Band. Produced by Alvin Ranglin.

Few singers have sold as many records in the reggae market as Gregory Isaacs. Reported substance abuse and changes in his voice caused by the loss of teeth have done little to dent his popularity, while a spell in prison on gun charges in the late 1980s only meant that he returned determined to score more hits then ever, by recording for virtually every producer around.

Born in 1951 in Kingston, Gregory started his career in the late 1960s with "Another Heartache", which disappeared without trace. A couple of records with the Concords did little better. The producer Rupie Edwards then voiced him solo, on singles like "Too Late"and "Lonely Man". Gregory's success in entering the Jamaican charts with "All I Have Is Love" in 1973, for Phil Pratt, helped to finance the African Museum label, started with another struggling singer, Errol Dunkley. His first release on the imprint, "Look Before You Leap", only sold moderately, but later gained classic status. That anticipated one side of his subsequent career – Gregory as the "sufferah", giving expression to his people's travails. "My Only Lover" was even more significant, providing the template for all the tunes on which he was to be cast as the vulnerable man hurt by love. Excellent singles for Gussie Clarke, Randy's, Roy Cousins, Dennis Alcapone and Glen Brown helped to consolidate his growing reputation.

His real breakthrough came when the Alvin 'GG' Ranglin-produced "Love Is Overdue" not only became one of Jamaica's best-selling records of 1974, but also topped the UK reggae chart. In the late 1970s, when 'rockers' rhythms ruled the dance-halls, Ranglin took Isaacs to the most popular studio in Kingston – the Hookim brothers' Channel One. Using rhythms by the Revolutionaries, Ranglin recorded the very successful *Best Of Gregory Isaacs* album, from which the **My Number One** set borrows five tracks. A further three tunes are lifted from the equally accomplished second volume that appeared three years later. The remaining tracks were originally released as singles on GG's label.

Of the hit singles from the vinyl albums, **My Number One** and **Border**, the former remains one of Isaacs' most popular love outings. Rather than cast the singer as the hurt lover, it has him simply cautious, asking to know the future plans of the girl who wants to be his "number one". As throughout the set, the delivery is deliciously cool, and the 12-inch mix means it segues into an excellent toast from Trinity, the "number one deejay". "Border" is also presented in its 12-inch form. Gregory's female audiences usually added vocal support on this tune, but here he's followed by the deejay U-Brown. A third chatter, Ranking Barnabas, adds his commentary to both **Tumbling Tears** and **Can I Change My Mind**, two tracks that make obvious the influence of Alton Ellis. **Philistines**, another popular single, is a declaration that Gregory intends to run rather than do any sentence. This was the first tune to express what was to become his characteristic paranoia – "One Man Against the World" was a later hit, providing the persona that took over from 'the cool ruler' and 'the lonely lover'.

At least ten Isaacs albums deserve a place in any reggae collection but there's no finer start than this, which showcases the Revolutionaries at their finest, has three deejays for variety, and a nice balance between lovers and cultural concerns.

⊃ We almost chose **Through The Years, Vols 1–3**, Jetstar, UK, 1997

Israel Vibration

The Same Song

Harvest, 1978, UK; Pressure Sounds, 1994, UK

Lascelles 'Wiss' Bulgin, Albert 'Apple' Craig and Cecil 'Skelly' Spencer (vocals).
Musicians include Mikey Chung (gtr, organ), Sly Dunbar (drums), Robbie
Shakespeare (bass). Produced by Tommy Cowan.

Israel Vibration – Lascelles 'Wiss' Bulgin, Albert 'Apple' Craig and Cecil 'Skelly' Spencer – came together firstly as friends, when they were patients at the Mona Heights Rehabilitation Centre in Kingston; they had all caught poliomyelitis in the epidemic that reached Jamaica in the 1950s. When they started to grow locks and smoke herb in the early 1970s, they were expelled from the institution. Apple told writer Eric Hiss in 1989: 'They help those who bow, and be the way they want them to be'. They lived rough, in the bush, finding that singing together enabled them to overcome their hunger pangs, albeit temporarily.

Eventually the trio became members of the 'bredrin' of the Rasta organization Twelve Tribes Of Israel, meeting a 'bredrin' named U Boot who financed a session for them at Treasure Isle studio. This resulted in their debut 45 **Why Worry**, and a deal with Tommy Cowan who recorded a second single, **The Same Song**, using members of Inner Circle, at that time backing Jacob Miller. The trio also performed live on Inner Circle shows at this time.

In 1978 Cowan released **The Same Song**, their debut album, on his Top Ranking label. He licensed the album to Harvest, a UK-based division of EMI previously known as a 'progressive' rock imprint. The set sold well in the crossover market that was being exploited by Island and Virgin with Bob Marley, Burning Spear and the Mighty Diamonds. The set fulfilled the promise shown on the 45s, with the trio's utterly natural harmonies – even if occasionally off-key – proving a perfect expression of the avowedly Rasta sentiments of the lyrics.

Although they sometimes showed traces of their influences – Burning Spear, Yabby You, Culture – Israel Vibration's vocal blend was very individual, and affecting in its unalloyed sincerity. Clearly the years of suffering with polio inculcated a quality of forbearance in the group, given focus by the teachings of the Twelve Tribes. Cowan re-recorded the first two singles for the album. The other songs were beautifully crafted reworkings of themes – life in Babylon (**Weep And Mourn**), Biblical prophecy (**Prophet Has Arise**), the goal of ultimate redemption (Jah **Time Has Come**) – by now common in reggae music. Cowan's version of **The Same Song**, a gently positive plea for unity among the various Rasta factions, is typical of the group sound. The CD cut included is longer than the original album cut, having previously appeared only as a 12-inch single.

After another three albums – dub sets *Israel Tafari* and *The Same Song Dub*, and the slightly more polished *Unconquered People*, the group ended their association with Cowan, going on to record for dancehall producer 'Junjo' Lawes, cutting the "Why You So Craven" set. That partnership, too, ended, and in 1983 the group relocated to the USA, recording again in 1987, when they began issuing albums for the Washington-based label Ras; these gained them a big following, particularly in the USA and France. The group split into two, Wiss and Skelly releasing *Pay The Piper* early in 1999, Apple going solo and issuing a solo album shortly after.

Looking back in 1989 Apple said: "Why [it] have to be that we have polio from such a tender age – why such hard things? We born innocent, pure to the world. But when we grow elder and start to realise, this was a purpose. There was a cause for us to be this way: music, message, prophecy. "Why Worry" demonstrates Apple's argument superbly.

➲ We almost chose **Unconquered People**, Greensleeves, UK, 1980

43

Linton Kwesi Johnson

Dread Beat An' Blood

Virgin, 1978, UK; Heartbeat, 1989, US/UK

Recorded 1977–78. Linton Kwesi Johnson (vocals and production).

Dub poetry – the recitation of verse over rhythms mixed in dub fashion – was developed at roughly the same time by poets both in Jamaica like Oku Onuora and Michael Smith, and in the UK like Linton Kwesi Johnson. An avowedly 'conscious' form, its progenitors include the celebrated Jamaican poet, writer and broadcaster Louise Bennett, US artists like the Last Poets and Gil Scott Heron, and sound system deejays in the Jamaican dancehall. Purists have occasionally dismissed it, but dub poetry at its best is a powerful, energizing experience. **Dread Beat An' Blood** signalled the arrival of the sub-genre in no uncertain terms, with Linton Kwesi Johnson dropping serious polemical arguments over Dennis Bovell's insinuating dub mixes.

LKJ, who was himself of Jamaican origin, born in August 1952 in Chapelton, Clarendon, came to the UK at the age of eleven. In his own words, "thirsty for knowledge", he attended Tulse Hill Secondary School in Brixton. After leaving school in 1970, he joined the Black Panther Party, and studied for a BA in Sociology at the University of London. In the Panthers he worked with Rasta Love, a group of poets and drummers, to organize a poetry workshop. In 1973 his own poems appeared in the journal *Race Today* and the magazine collective published his first two poetry collections, *The Voices Of The Living And The Dead* in 1974, and *Dread Beat And Blood* in 1975. The Arts Council used the latter name as the title for a film, shown on the

BBC, and also supported poetry programmes in Johnson's home borough of Lambeth. When he began experimenting with reggae bands at his readings, he was the borough's official writer-in-residence. For Johnson, poetry wasn't passive; his poems, usually cast in a written version of Jamaican spoken patois, and delivered matter-of-factly with little tonal variation, were designed to address the real issues – racism, police brutality, the failings of 'justice' – then facing working-class black people in the UK. As an active member of *Race Today*, Johnson read his poems at demonstrations as well as formal readings.

When LKJ signed with Virgin in 1977, they first released the single **It Dread Inna Inglan** – Johnson's response to the arrest and imprisonment of a man named George Lindo, forced by police to sign a false confession – under the name 'Poet and the Roots'. Similarly, **Man Free** commemorates *Race Today* editor Darcus Howe's release from prison after one week of a sentence for assault on a (white) barrister.

Other songs depict the dancehall culture of the UK Jamaican community. He celebrates it on the title track, dramatically evokes and criticizes its negative aspects – gang war – on **Five Nights Of Bleeding**, and links these events to class oppression in wider society on **Doun De Road**. Bassist and guitarist Vivian Weathers contributes an anguished vocal, in the manner of Prince Lincoln, to **Song Of Blood**; the stark lyric of **Come Wi Goh Dung Deh** is delivered by LKJ almost in a conventional deejay style. Its lyric – simple but intensely political – seems to be about Jamaica, but could apply to any underdeveloped post-colonial country; the piece ends with an understated dub section. The final track, an eloquent summary of his politics, indicates LKJ's major direction over his next three albums, all released on Island between 1979 and 1984.

These days, LKJ runs his own label and publishing house, and continues to be active in poetry, dub or otherwise. While his 1990s albums reveal a more personal, subjective voice, his political principles are expressed as sharply as ever.

➲ We almost chose **Independent Intavenshun (Anthology)**, Island, 1998

44

Dave Kelly/Various Artists

Pepper Seed Jam!

Mad House, 1995, UK

Recorded 1995. Produced by Dave 'Rude Boy' Kelly. Artists include Terror Fabulous, Buju Banton, Chippie Ranks, Spragga Benz, Louie Culture, Wayne Wonder, Daddy Screw, General Degree, Nadine Sutherland, Donovan Steele.

As both musician and first-class engineer, Dave 'Rude Boy' Kelly played a major role in the success of Donovan Germain's Penthouse studio at 56 Slipe Pen Road, next door to Gussie Clarke's Music Works in Kingston 5. Using facilities at Penthouse, he launched his own Mad House label in 1992, following Buju Banton's "Big it Up" single by the same deejay's commentary on the dancehall fashion for ultra-brief shorts, "Batty Rider". Both Jamaican hits employed the sort of minimal drum-based rhythms that were to be Kelly's trademark, and became the most important shift in reggae since the music had gone digital. Another important hit in both Jamaica and the UK was "Action", a 'combination' effort from up-and-coming deejay Terror Fabulous and the established singer Nadine Sutherland, which again emphasized drum beats rather than the traditional bass line. The "Pepper Seed" rhythm in 1995 took the trend another leap forward, with a catchy keyboard figure providing virtually the only melody over the mesmerizing and radical drum pattern.

In common with virtually every popular modern rhythm, "Pepper Seed" was eventually given an album of its own, **Pepper Seed Jam!** For the benefit of anyone unfamiliar with the conventions of the modern Jamaican dancehall, the 'one-rhythm' or 'version' album is made up entirely of different cuts – from deejays or singers – of the same rhythm track. A uniquely Jamaican phenomenon, it's an important component of a market that remains largely singles-oriented.

Such albums can, of course, be hard going unless you are totally enamoured of the rhythm in question; and even then, when the mixes and performances aren't sufficiently varied, ten or twelve versions can just seem to confirm the old adage about all reggae sounding the same. Though its history can be traced back to Rupie Edwards' *Yamaha Skank* set in the early 1970s, the sub-genre came into its own during the computerized ragga era, when almost every hit rhythm was deemed worthy of its own 'version' set. With the first 'megamix' album, the young Dave Kelly took the form to its logical conclusion.

Kelly's innovative "Pepper Seed" rhythm had already created some serious dancehall excitement. Of at least half a dozen versions that appeared as 7-inch singles, Spragga Benz's **Things Ah Gwaan**, Terror Fabulous' **Yuh Nuh Kotch/Number 2**, and Daddy Screw and Donovan Steele's **Big Things** made the strongest impact. Instead of the conventional 'version' album, placing ten separate cuts alongside each other, Kelly came up with something a little different. Drawing inspiration from the dancehall practice of 'juggling' (or mixing) tracks on twin turntables, as developed by leading sounds like Stone Love, he segued them together to form one seamless piece of music. These were also edited down for the mix, so that no fewer than 26 tracks could be included – with deejay, vocal and 'combination' cuts not so much in competition as complementing each other. Even slightly earlier Mad House hits, like Terror Fabulous and Nadine Sutherland's **Action** and cultural deejay Louie Culture's **Bogus Badge**, appeared with the new drum beats grafted on.

If you wanted to check out just a single one-rhythm album, you couldn't do better than Dave Kelly's first ground-breaking experiment – both for the performances, and for the truly infectious rhythm.

⊃ We almost chose **John Crow By The Fireside**, Penthouse, US, 1996

45

King Tubby

Dub Gone Crazy

Blood & Fire, 1994, UK

Recorded 1975–79. King Tubby (engineer). Also engineered by Philip Smart, Prince Jammy and Hopeton 'Scientist' Brown. Produced by Bunny Lee.

Producer Bunny 'Striker' Lee was a pivotal figure in the development of the 'version' in Jamaican music. Born in 1941, he was producing successful rock steady in the late 1960s, but it was during the next era that he really made his mark, and helped to shape the future course of reggae. Other producers had already released instrumental and deejay versions of vocal tunes, while the engineers who mixed the first dub sides for commercial release, King Tubby and Errol 'ET' Thompson, had sat at the mixing boards for pioneering albums from Lee Perry and Randy's. Producers Herman Chin-Loy and Prince Buster had issued their own sets. However, it was Striker who not only popularized dub, but also, by his sheer number of 'versions', most anticipated the dancehall revolution of the 1980s.

Lacking facilities of his own, the ever-resourceful Bunny Lee cut expensive studio time by two means: he had his session band record vintage rhythms they already knew, and then put as many different singers and deejays over the tracks as the market would stand. It was an approach that always ran the risk of seeming formulaic, but for the fact that he was among the first producers to employ the services of Osbourne Ruddock, aka King Tubby, for the stunning remixes on the flip sides.

King Tubby had already received credits on the dubs of a U-Roy single for Glen Brown, and a couple of Larry Marshall hits for Carlton Patterson. However, Striker was the first producer to put out a full dub set under Tubby's name, and *Dub Master: Dub From The Roots* – with its cover photograph of the regal engineer – set the trend for making the man at the mixing board the featured star. Predictably, its success in the reggae marketplace resulted in Tubby's dubbing several more sets of Striker's rhythms into oblivion. But at least as important as the albums were the version sides of 45s, usually bearing a credit to King Tubby, and appetizing titles like "This A the Hardest Version". Often the record buyer wouldn't have to hear the top side: just the thought of an accompanying dub mixed at Tubby's studio was enough.

The **Dub Gone Crazy** collection, which is appropriately subtitled "The Evolution of Dub at King Tubby's", features dub sides from rare singles plus unreleased dub mixes from Striker's master tapes. Although it was not released until 1994, it gains from its retrospective nature. While even the better dub albums from the time tend to have a couple of weak tracks, here only the Aggrovators' hardest rhythms were chosen, along with the most imaginative mixes – not just from Tubby himself, but also his disciples, Philip Smart, Prince Jammy and Hopeton 'Scientist' Brown.

Interesting as it is to try and distinguish the individual styles of the engineers – and it's not that easy – no amount of mixing virtuosity can hide a weak rhythm. It's partly the quality of the original tracks from Striker that ensures interest is maintained throughout. Making full use of slide fader, phase shifter, echo and equalization, these are all dubs that impress in their own right. But the voices that come in and out of most of the mixes should prompt many more people to look for the full vocals of, say, Johnny Clarke's "Death In The Arena", Leroy Smart's "Wreck Up My Life", Barry Brown's "Live It Up Youthman" or Wayne Jarrett's "Satta Dread". As an overview of the inspired work done at the studio at 18 Dromilly Avenue, this is perhaps the best place for the newcomer to either Tubby's mixing board or Striker's production style to start.

➲ We almost chose **Dub Gone 2 Crazy**, Blood & Fire, UK, 1996

46

Barrington Levy

Collection

Greensleeves, 1990, UK

Recorded 1979–88. Barrington Levy (vocals). Produced by Henry 'Junjo' Lawes and Hyman 'Jah Life' Wright.

Mention of the dancehall period of the early 1980s usually brings to mind a plethora of deejays, but the first performer to record an album with the producer and session band who most defined the era was the teenage singing sensation Barrington Levy. On that debut album, *Bounty Hunter*, Barrington unleashed his vibrant vocal attack over a series of raw rhythms built by musicians then credited as the Channel One All Stars, who were shortly to be known as the Roots Radics.

The impact of the set, in the final year of the 1970s, was comparable to that of the Mighty Diamonds' *Right Time*, recorded at the same studio four years previously, which had established the all-pervasive rockers sound of Sly Dunbar and the Revolutionaries. Jointly produced by Henry 'Junjo' Lawes and the New York-based Hyman 'Jah Life' Wright, *Bounty Hunter* was to be the template for the whole genre of dancehall vocalizing, and Lawes dominated the Kingston dancehalls for the next five years.

Born in Kingston in 1964, young Barrington recorded with the Mighty Multitudes group in 1977, and made a couple of unsuccessful solo discs, before he linked up with Junjo and Hyman for the first of his many hit singles – "Ah Ya We Deh". This spirited effort was followed by the even more popular "Callie Weed", "Looking My Love" and **Shine Eye Gal**, and when his debut album arrived from New York it was snapped up in all the world's reggae capitals. **Bounty Hunter** itself kicked things off, immediately informing listeners that there had been another fundamental shift in the music, and it also starts **Collection**, a career-spanning compilation of Levy's work when he first emerged, the excitement and energy he exuded seeming to owe everything to current dancehall practices – particularly the manner in which deejays would fling down lyrics over whatever revived Studio One rhythm was calling the shots.

Two more equally strong tracks from that ground-breaking first album, "Shine Eye Gal" and **Don't Fuss Or Fight**, come next. Sadly, space wasn't found for "It's Not Easy" (aka "Looking My Love"), Barrington's cut of the enduring "Real Rock" rhythm. To make up for that omission, there are a brace of killer Junjo productions from a couple of years later – **Mary Long Tongue**, and the singer's devastating cut of the Wailing Souls' "Waterhouse Rock", **Prison Oval Rock**. His account of how cash circulates, **Money Move**, is not the hit single from George Phang, but an interesting enough alternative cut of the lyric, part-produced by Jah Screw. A better-known outing from the same producer, **Under Mi Sensi**, pays tribute to Junjo's sound system, Volcano, and that set's renown selector, Danny Dread. Jah Screw was also responsible for the rock-influenced (but totally successful) **Here I Come**, on which Barrington declares how he's "broader than Broadway" and two marvellous restylings of vintage Jamaican hits – **Step Up In Life**, based on Toot Hibbert's "Pomps & Pride" (with an uncredited deejay), and **Too Experienced**, his very successful version of the Bob Andy song, which suggests one of the influences on his phrasing.

Inevitably, this compilation misses some classics – such as "Revelation" for Dennis Star, "My Woman" for Joe Gibbs, "Murder" for Hyman Wright and Percy Chin, "Praise His Name" for George Phang, and "Like Soldier" for Channel One – but until someone presents the deserved boxed set, drawing on Levy's work for a dozen or more producers, it will have to do.

⮕ We almost chose **Too Experienced: Best Of...**, VP, US, 1998

47

Lone Ranger

On The Other Side Of Dub

Heartbeat, 1991, US

Recorded 1978-79; Lone Ranger (deejay). Produced by Coxsone Dodd.

The art of talking over rhythm tracks – MC-ing, toasting, chanting, deejaying and rapping – has been practised in Jamaican dancehalls for fifty years, but it was in the early 1970s that it really took off on disc, with U-Roy – 'The Originator'. After him hundreds picked up the mike to fling down lyrics on sound systems and in studios. The early years were dominated by U-Roy and Big Youth, who in turn inspired such as Dillinger and Trinity, and then, as the decade drew to a close, names like Michigan & Smiley, General Echo, Ranking Joe, and Lone Ranger emerged from the vibrant dance scene.

Unlike the earlier days, no single deejay really controlled the dancehall. In fact, given dancehall conditions, establishing who originated what style first is almost impossible. Deejays borrowed lyrics and patterns freely from each other, refining them further in sessions. Probably the most influential figures were Echo, for his style and his choice of outrageously slack subject matter, and Ranking Joe, who was more of a link between U-Roy and the new 'fast style' of the 1980s. Lone Ranger (born Anthony Waldron) was without question another major player – and a deejay whose stylistic followers included the slack Johnny Ringo and the extremely popular Yellowman. He was (and still is) one of the best in the business at improvising witty lyrics that blended local themes, cartoon-inspired fantasy, street slang and time-honoured phrases, which he punctuated with assorted trills and yelps. He delivered this mix of culture, slackness, and gun lyrics in a style that echoed the masters.

Ranger started off at Studio One in 1978–79, for whom he recorded a great series of singles – including a version of Slim Smith's "Never Let Go" rhythm ("The Answer") that gained him attention – and also recorded with Welton Irie, later his fellow deejay on Virgo Hi-Fi, champion sound of 1980. He linked up with producer Leon Synmoie, owner of the Thrillseekers label, for his first huge hit, "Barnabas Collins".

On The Other Side Of Dub, his first Studio One album, sums up what a major part of this explosion of deejay talent was all about. It was released by Coxsone in 1981 but had probably been in the can for a while as it predates his biggest hit, "Love Bump". For the album's CD reissue, Heartbeat added a previously unreleased version of Barnabas Collins, a tale of a vampire who wakes in search of a pretty neck to bite. The original hit rode a cut of Slim Smith's "Conversation"; this version uses Studio One's cut of the Techniques "You Don't Care".

The other tracks – as on the original vinyl – comprise five toasts and five tough dub versions mixed by Coxsone. Standout tracks include Quarter Pound Ishen (on the Royals "Pick Up The Pieces"), where he both nods to U-Roy and adapts lyrics made famous by Ranking Joe on champion sound Ray Symbolic. Everything She Want rides a cut of the "Drifter" rhythm; the lyrics deal with a girl who borrows clothes, a subject still with us today. Noah In The Ark uses Ernest Wilson's "Why Oh Why" to deliver a cultural theme; Natty Dread On The Go has Coxsone's cut of the Wailers' "Hypocrite". The corresponding dub cuts will appeal to anyone with a taste for the Brentford Road style of mixing – which invariably draws attention to something different in the rhythms.

Ranger went on to be one of the most successful deejays of the early 1980s but in mid-decade he relocated to the USA, without advancing his career significantly. He returned to Jamaica in late 1998, and has since begun deejaying sound system again; even better, his old abilities are seemingly intact.

➲ We almost chose **Lone Ranger Collection**, Grapevine, UK, 1995

48

Luciano

Where There Is Life

Island Jamaica, 1995, UK

Recorded 1994–95. Luciano (vocals). Produced by Phillip 'Fatis' Burrell.

If the late Garnett Silk was the Jamaican vocalist who most clearly signalled the return to roots and culture in the early 1990s, then in terms of both talent and popularity Luciano has been the most important figure since. Born Jepther McClymont in Davey Town in 1974, he cut his first records in 1992, for Hertnol 'Sky High' Henry and Castro Brown. Promising enough modern roots efforts, they perhaps showed his main influences – Dennis Brown, Frankie Paul and Stevie Wonder – a little too plainly.

However, the young singer's tunes of the following year, for both Freddie McGregor's Big Ship label and Phillip 'Fatis' Burrell's Xterminator, showed that he had matured to find his own, beautifully controlled voice. Freddie McGregor tended to concentrate on the singer's 'lovers' side, scoring Luciano his first number one in the UK reggae charts with the blues-dance favourite 'Shake It Up Tonight', which served as the title for a splendid (albeit underrated) album. Fatis, on the other hand, chose to develop the cultural approach with which Luciano has become most identified, impressing initially with strong 45s such as "Chant Out", "Poor and Simple" and "Black Survivors".

The success of these early tunes on Xterminator led to a contract with Island, and the classic **Where There Is Life** album in the summer of 1995. This thoughtful cultural collection was obviously designed to set Luciano apart from the other new

Jamaican singers then concentrating on 'real' songs (as opposed to stringing together dancehall catch phrases). It counts as one of reggae's defining moments, on its own terms comparable to *Talking Book* or even *What's Going On*.

Unlike Luciano's first – admittedly very strong – album for the producer, *Where There Is Life* was meant to be far more than an anthology of proven 45s. Instead it was conceived as an album, whose sum is even greater than its individual parts. The reflective **It's Me Again Jah** had topped both the Jamaican and UK reggae charts the previous year, and its relaxed, dignified feel carried over to the rest of this exceptionally well-crafted set. Yet though Luciano's output for Fatis had been prolific – no less than eight singles were released simultaneously at one point in 1994 – none of the singer's other previous 45s were included. Three tracks appeared as singles only after the album – the beguiling **Who Could It Be**, **Your World and Mine**, and his 'combination' tune with 'conscious' deejay Louie Culture, **In This Together**.

As witnessed by titles like **He Is My Friend**, **Lord Give Me Strength**, and **Heaven Help Us All**, the entire set was rooted in Luciano's faith, but the utter passion with which he tackled such themes prevented a slide into mere religiosity. There was also the matter of the beautifully melodic but tough Xterminator rhythms – built by such Kingston studio stalwarts as Sly Dunbar and Robbie Shakespeare on drums and bass, keyboards player Robbie Lynn, and saxophonist Dean Frazer.

Though its immediate follow-up, *The Messenger*, was slightly disappointing, Mr McClymont's subsequent Burrell-produced album, **Sweep Over My Soul**, was a stunning return to form. He clearly still has a lot more to offer, as has been borne out by his first serious forays into freelancing. Noteworthy tunes have appeared on a variety of Jamaican labels, including Henfield, Raggey Joe, Jahmento, Jazzy Creation, Flash and Bobby Digital's Brick Wall. That said, Luciano's records for Fatis will always be worth returning to, and none more so than this landmark in modern roots music.

➲ We almost chose **Sweep Over My Soul**, Jetstar, UK, 1999

49

Bob Marley and the Wailers

Songs Of Freedom

Island, 1992, US/UK

Recorded 1962–83. The Wailers: Bob Marley (vocals), Peter Tosh (vocals), Bunny Wailer (vocals). Producers include Coxsone Dodd, Leslie Kong, Lee Perry, Johnny Nash, Chris Blackwell, Alex Sadkin, The Wailers.

Reputedly the biggest-selling CD box set in history (at 1.2m copies and rising), **Songs Of Freedom** provides a definitive overview of the career of reggae's biggest, indeed only, global superstar, Robert Nesta Marley (1945–81), whose name remains synonymous with reggae two decades after his death from cancer. In 78 selections, it ranges from Marley's 1962 debut, **Judge Not**, through to a rendition of **Redemption Song** from his very last performance at Pittsburgh in September 1980. His music during those years can be divided into two stages. In the first, the focus is on the foundation and survival of the Wailers, and their early efforts on the local Jamaican scene; in the second, international phase, Bob Marley is the main figure.

The details of Marley's life – his attempts to get into the music business, meeting the other Wailers, their subsequent apprenticeship, and eventual rise to fame – are outlined in a 64-page booklet. There's a preface from wife Rita and contributions from former associates, together with a track commentary and partial sessionography, all of which adds in no small measure to an understanding of the legend behind the music.

What it reveals is that, talented as Bob Marley was, he couldn't have achieved what he did without a lot of help. This came initially from Jamaican producers like Clement Dodd, more importantly from Lee Perry, and equally from musicians such as bassist Aston 'Family Man' Barrett. Lastly, without Chris Blackwell and the international record company he had founded, Marley would have never been able to project his strong and coherent musical vision to the world beyond Jamaica.

The first ten years are summarized on discs one and two. As Marley pays his dues, the songs move from ska through not-quite-typical rock steady to early reggae. Highlights include productions from the Wailers' own Wail M Soul M outfit: the much-versioned **Hypocrites**, the first cut of **Stir It Up**, and the moving **Thank You Lord**. The best Leslie Kong-produced side – the joyous **Soul Shakedown Party** – is also here, as are crucial cuts produced by Lee Perry, who guided the Wailers as they made the transition from vocal trio to a more progressive, militant style. **Small Axe**, **Duppy Conqueror**, and **Soul Rebel** formed a blueprint for much of Marley's later work with Island.

A stunning acoustic medley is next, recorded by Marley in a hotel room in Stockholm in 1971, when employed as a songwriter for Johnny Nash. It again prefigures his later output, like a revelatory pencil sketch of a future masterpiece. The remaining two and a half CDs concentrate on his Island output, without overly conflicting with material on his dozen sets for the label. Much has not appeared on album before – 12-inch mixes, live versions and titles only released in Jamaica. The anthology, overall, proves that Bob Marley's achievement is unlikely to be superseded by any single reggae artist. These are the songs and performances that made him a genuine superstar, particularly in the so-called third world. He spoke unequivocally for those masses, universalizing their concerns for the rest of the planet. They understood him best of all: he truly was a son of the ghetto who never lost sight of his roots there. *Songs of Freedom* is absolutely essential.

➲ We almost chose **Soul Revolution 1 & 2**, Trojan, UK, 1989

50

Larry Marshall

Presenting Larry Marshall

Heartbeat, 1992, US

Recorded c. 1968–73. Larry Marshall (vocals) with Eric Frater (gtr), Leroy Sibbles (bass), Jackie Mittoo (organ), and others. Produced by Coxsone Dodd.

According to his own account, the young Larry Marshall (born Fitzroy Marshall, St Ann's, Jamaica, 1945) arrived in Kingston from the country in 1957 – a couple of years before the birth of the Jamaican recording industry. He nevertheless attended plenty of dances, where he heard sound systems pumping out r'n'b discs from the States at maximum volume. Around five years later, Larry was in a recording studio himself, making his first Jamaican hit, "Snake In the Grass", for the Chinese-Jamaican producer Justin Yap.

While his records on the Yap brothers' Top Deck and Tuneico labels gave him a name with Jamaican record buyers, they only hinted at Larry's full potential, which was realized when he moved to Studio One towards the close of the decade. Despite Dodd's lack of enthusiasm, Larry's first recording at Brentford Road, Nanny Goat, was a huge seller, and is often credited as one of the tunes to signal the shift from rock steady to reggae. Larry recorded his song, which was based on a rural proverb, with singing partner Alvin Leslie, and more classics credited to Larry and Alvin followed on various Studio One imprints.

His next move, to Carlton Patterson's Black & White set-up, resulted in the well-remembered "I Admire You". Its popular 'version' side, "Watergate Rock", was mixed at King Tubby's, as were "Not Responsible" and "Can't You Understand".

Subsequent self-produced work on his own Amanda label consolidated Larry's reputation as both singer and songwriter, as well as a wonderful arranger.

Coxsone released two variations of **Presenting Larry Marshall** on vinyl, and the Heartbeat CD draws from both. That means thirteen prime tracks, covering most of his best-known work for Coxsone, plus a dub version of his duet with Alton Ellis, **Wonderful World**, as a bonus. This inclusion of the dub is slightly odd, given that he recorded at least 28 sides at Brentford Road, with very little that wasn't of the highest rank. A pity that the rootsy "Press Along Nyah" or "Run Babylon" couldn't have been included, or the just as strong "Lonely Room", "Free I Lord", or "Your Love".

Given the quality of what is collected here, that's perhaps quibbling. The rhythms employed on several of the tracks, if not Larry's original vocals, will be familiar to anyone with even a passing interest in reggae. "Nanny Goat" and **Throw Me Corn** are certainly the most famous. The former provided further hits on Studio One in the form of Dennis Alcapone's "Forever Version" and the Sound Dimension's instrumental "Musical Scorcher", before becoming a dancehall staple. The latter resurfaced initially as the deejay Charlie Ace's "Father and Dreadlocks", but came into its own in the 1980s, when producers like George Phang, Gussie Clarke and King Jimmy treated it to version after version, and Dodd responded by dusting off the original rhythm track for the Ethiopians' "Muddy Water" and Horace Andy's "Slacky Tidy". The beautifully insistent rhythm of **Mean Girl**, too, lived on in further Studio One cuts, including early tunes by Little Joe and Prince Far I, but became best known when masterfully refashioned at Channel One for the Mighty Diamonds' "I Need A Roof".

However often the rhythms for Larry Marshall's Studio One classics are recycled, there is no substitute for hearing the writer of some of the most heartfelt songs ever to emerge from Jamaica. Pray that Heartbeat, or Dodd himself, can be persuaded to release another set to complement this marvellous introduction.

➲ We almost chose **I Admire You**, Heartbeat, US/UK, 1992

51

The Maytals

Time Tough: the Anthology

Island Jamaica/Chronicles,1996, US

Recorded 1963–88. The Maytals: Frederick 'Toots' Hibbert (vocals), Henry 'Raleigh'
Gordon (backing vocals), Nathaniel 'Jerry' Mathias (backing vocals). Producers
include Coxsone Dodd, Prince Buster, Bunny Lee, Victor Chin, Leslie Kong, Warrick
Lynn, Chris Blackwell, Alex Sadkin, Toots Hibbert, Sly Dunbar, Jim Dickinson.

Frederick 'Toots' Hibbert is one
artist who definitely deserves a
multiple-CD box set. While several Maytals compilations are on
the market, they vary in sound
quality, and some are of dubious
legality; only Prince Buster has
been worse served by reissues.
Happily, Island's two-CD **Time
Tough** anthology manages to
touch most of the high points of a
career that has so far lasted four decades.

Although Toots started out as a solo singer – he cut a dubplate
for sound system owner King Edwards the Giant in 1961 – his
career only took off when he teamed up with backing singers
Jerry Mathias and Raleigh Gordon, to form the Maytals. Taking
their name from Toots' hometown of May Pen, they sang a sanc-
tified style of ska that could only have had its origins in a Baptist
church. The success of their first record for Coxsone Dodd,
"Hallelujah" – which harnessed a revivalist feel to the driving ska
laid down by the future Skatalites – set the pattern for further
Coxsone discs, interspersing Baptist knees-ups with lugubrious
soul-style ballads. Toot's fiery vocals, and the insistent 'African'
call-and-response patterns, proved very popular.

After a couple of dozen titles for Dodd and little in the way of
remuneration, the trio moved on to other producers, including

Beverley's, Kentone and Randy's. This period saw them established as the premier vocal group of ska, a position they consolidated with Prince Buster via numerous singles – **Broadway Jungle** among them – and a solitary album.

The group next cut an album for Byron Lee, as well as the 1966 Song Festival winner, "Bam Bam", before Toots spent a short term in jail for possession of herb. On his release, the Maytals began recording for Leslie Kong in the new reggae style. A string of hits followed, fifty-plus titles that rank among the greatest vocal group performances in Jamaican music history. Notable among them were Toots' celebratory **54-46 That's My Number**, and **Do The Reggay** (sic), the first song to feature that word in its title. They're here alongside classics like **Pressure Drop**, **She's My Scorcher**, **Sweet and Dandy**, and **Monkey Man** (the nearest the Maytals got to a UK chart hit).

After Leslie Kong's death in 1971, Toots linked up with his associate Warrick Lynn, and Chris Blackwell, then searching for a reggae act to present to the rock audience. Blackwell saw Toots as a great soul singer, and prompted him to move in that direction. Each new Toots album thereafter featured soul-influenced as well as traditional reggae, and covers drawn from beyond Jamaica. This culminated in 1988's well-received *Toots in Memphis* set, on which Memphis musicians such as Al Green's guitarist Teenie Hodges and Andrew Love of the Memphis Horns play alongside Jamaican counterparts like Sly Dunbar and Robbie Shakespeare. As well as Otis Redding standards like **I've Got Dreams To Remember** and **Hard To Handle**, there's a superb version of Jackie Moore's **Precious Precious**.

Toots Hibbert still tours regularly, his powers apparently undiminished. A definitive edition of his Kong-produced Beverley's material – at least a three-CD set – is sorely needed, while the Prince Buster ska material, and many early-1970s titles, have also yet to appear on CD. In their absence, this forty-track summary provides an ideal starting point and proof, for the unconverted, of his huge talents and legendary status.

➲ We almost chose **Never Grow Old**, Heartbeat, US/UK, 1997

52

Freddie McGregor

Bobby Bobylon

Studio One, 1980, JA; Heartbeat, 1991, US

Recorded 1979–80. Freddie McGregor (vocals). Produced by Coxsone Dodd.

Jamaican singers and deejays often start to perform at remarkably young ages; Freddie McGregor is just one of many reputed to have stood on an orange crate in order to reach the mike at Studio One. Be that as it may, he was born in 1956 in Clarendon, so he must have been about ten years old when he sang "Do Good", "Why Did My Little Girl Cry", and "Why Did You Do It" with Ernest 'Fitzy' Wilson of the Clarendonians in the late ska era. By his teens, he was playing drums on Studio One sessions, and impressing with solo records like "Children Listen To Wise Words", Go Away Pretty Girl, and a cover of Junior Byles' "Beat Down Babylon".

In the mid-1970s, McGregor joined the Twelve Tribes of Israel, and made the cultural statements "I Man A Rasta" and Rastaman Camp, still two of his most enduring tunes. From 1977 onwards, he worked with other producers, but worthwhile tracks continued to appear on Studio One. Strong material was also cut with Earl Smith's Soul Syndicate band, including "Revolutionist" (a restyling of "I Man A Rasta"), the very heavy "Mark Of the Beast", "Natural Collie", and a version of George Benson's "Love Ballad". A powerful debut album with the Soul Syndicate, *Mr McGregor*, was produced by Niney the Observer.

"Big Ship", his biggest hit for Linval Thompson, gave the name for McGregor's own label, launched in 1984 with the excellent "Across the Border" single. In the 1990s, he has continued to release superb records on Big Ship, including the very popular *Sings Jamaican Favourites* series of albums, as well as issuing outstanding singles on labels like Steely and Clevie, Fat Eyes, Xterminator and Mister Tipsy.

Despite a professional relationship that went back to the first half of the 1960s, Clement Dodd didn't exactly rush out Freddie's first album for Studio One. When **Bobby Bobylon** finally appeared in 1980, a year after Niney had issued the singer's debut set, it had obviously been worth the wait. A superbly packaged set, it featured five of his singles reworked to even greater effect, a striking cover of the Ethiopians' **Gonna Take Over Now**, and well-crafted new songs placed over old rhythms. **Bobby Bobylon** itself employed the rhythm from Jackie Mittoo's classic instrumental, "One Step Beyond", which had already provided the title track for Dodd's *Hi Fashion Dub* album. Versioning of the track began in earnest after Freddie's cut, with such examples as Barrington Levy's "Money Move" and Frankie Paul's "Tidal Wave" hits for George Phang. **Bandulo** utilized a far more obscure rhythm – the Soul Invaders' "Soulful Music" – in equally memorable fashion.

To the great relief of listeners used to hearing Studio One classics given inappropriate remixes, both Freddie's Rastafarian anthems, "Rastaman Camp" and **I Am A Revolutionist**, lost none of their power through being significantly updated. Similarly, "Go Away Pretty Girl" and **What Difference Does It Make**, if anything, improved upon the originals, with bright new mixes designed for contemporary dancehall play. The fresh **Wine Of Violence** and **We Need Love** – versions respectively of Ernest Wilson's "Undying Love" and the Kingstonians' "I Make A Woman" – were easily of the same exalted calibre. Freddie's thoughtful words on the violence that had been destabilizing Jamaica in the late 1970s were grafted seamlessly onto remixes of the vintage rhythms. This exceptionally gifted singer has recorded several albums of the highest quality since this, but for heartfelt freshness this is the one to investigate first.

➲ We almost chose **Sings Jamaican Favourites Vol. 2**, VP, US, 1992

53

The Melodians

Swing and Dine

Heartbeat, 1992, US/UK

Recorded 1966–74. The Melodians: Brent Dowe (vocals), Tony Brevette (vocals), Trevor McNaughton (vocals). Produced by Sonia Pottinger and Duke Reid.

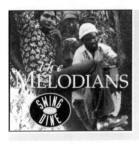

The way the musical style of US r'n'b and soul groups like the Drifters, the Temptations, and the Impressions was reinterpreted in Jamaica is typified by the work of such groups as the Blues Busters, the Paragons, the Techniques, and the Melodians. The latter group – Brent 'Porky' Dowe, Tony Brevette, Trevor McNaughton, and writing member Ranford Cogle – first got together in 1962, entering talent competitions. They also participated in all-night singing sessions held in the Kingston ghetto location 'Back O'Wall' (now Tivoli Gardens). Along with singers like Ken Boothe, Stranger Cole, Slim Smith, Roy Shirley and Jimmy Riley, they'd rehearse and practise in the open air, inspired by the sound systems playing in the same area.

By 1965, the Melodians were ready to record. Following the standard trajectory, they started out at Studio One, cutting "Lay It On" and three other songs in their first session. Hearing that Duke Reid paid more money, they soon moved to Treasure Isle, where they made I'll Get Along Without You and You Don't Need Me. Those hits, and most of their subsequent smashes for Reid, are featured on the **Swing and Dine** compilation, along with tracks recorded for Jamaica's only woman producer of note, Mrs Sonia Pottinger.

The Melodians' brief stint with Leslie Kong's Beverley's imprint in the early 1970s, during which they cut the international bestsellers "Rivers Of Babylon" and "Sweet Sensation", was ended by Kong's premature death. Returning to Mrs Pottinger, they gained hits with It's All In The Family and I'll Take You Where The Music's Playing.

Dowe and Brevette then embarked on moderately successful solo careers, which faded by the early 1980s Brevette released self-productions such as "Don't Get Weary" and a version of Curtis Mayfield's "Need To Belong", while Dowe scored on a series of hits for Pottinger, including "Build Me Up", "Close To You" and a remake of Alton Ellis's "Girl I've Got A Date". Dowe also recorded for Lee Perry, Bunny Lee, and Tommy Cowan, as well as on his own account, and found time to produce the Greenwich Farm vocal group, the Palmer Brothers, on their classic roots anthem "Stepping Out Of Babylon" in 1976.

Whereas most groups rely on one lead singer, the Melodians were blessed with two: the warm baritone of Tony Brevette and the soulful, demonstrative tenor of Brent Dowe. Both remain underrated to this day. *Swing and Dine* shows them to be never less than top-class, delivering a beautifully realized blend of lead vocals and ensemble singing. Brevette is absolutely outstanding on the Reid productions Come On Little Girl, "I Know Just How She Feels" (here retitled Far Away Love) and "You Don't Need Me". He is similarly outstanding on the Pottinger hits Little Nut Tree – a near perfect adaptation of a nursery song – and the Drifters' "I'll Take You Where The Music's Playing".

Dowe sings lead on the bulk of the other tracks, though they alternate on the dancehall anthem Swing and Dine. An added delight is the work of the session bands, with guitarist Lynn Taitt proving that he was the master of rock steady guitar. In recent years the original Melodians trio has made a well-received return, appearing on 'revival' shows in Jamaica and the UK. Happily, these performances have shown the group's vocal abilities to be intact and their song canon, expressing a combination of sincerity and innocence, as strong as ever.

⮕ We almost chose **Various: Musical Feast**, Heartbeat, US/UK, 1991

54

Mighty Diamonds

Go Seek Your Rights

Virgin, 1990, UK

Recorded 1976–78. The Mighty Diamonds: Donald 'Tabby' Shaw, Fitzroy 'Bunny' Simpson and Lloyd 'Judge' Ferguson. Produced by Joseph Hookim and Karl Pitterson.

Early in 1975, when the Mighty Diamonds vocal trio exploded onto the Jamaican scene, with a series of hits on the Channel One subsidiary Well Charge, they appeared to have come from nowhere. In fact, however, they had started as protegés of producer Pat Francis (aka deejay Jah Lloyd) in 1969, and Greenwich Farm impresario Tony Mack had featured them on his talent shows during the early 1970s. Around that time, the trio cut "Girl You Are Too Young" and "Oh No Baby" for Stranger Cole, and "Mash Up" for Derrick Harriott. Over the next couple of years, they made a handful of titles for other producers, sweetly sung in Jamaican soul style. These included discs for the Rosseblimo label and for Bunny Lee ("Jah Jah Bless The Dreadlocks" and "Carefree Girl"), plus "Talk About It" for Lee Perry. However, it was the excellent Shame and Pride for Jah Lloyd that first gained them attention.

The Mighty Diamonds' arrival at Jo Jo Hookim's Channel One in 1975 was serendipitous; the studio was about to become the dominant Jamaican recording location. The harmonies of Donald Shaw, Fitzroy Simpson, and Lloyd Ferguson were thrown into sharp relief over the militant rockers updates of classic rhythms then being created by the Revolutionaries, propelled by the dynamic drum and bass duo of Sly Dunbar and Robbie

Shakespeare. The subject matter of their songs also underwent a dramatic shift. Although the Diamonds started off with covers of Stylistics songs like "Hey Girl" and "Country Living", they soon applied their sweet harmonizing to reality lyrics and Garvey-inspired themes. Starting with "Back Weh" in late 1975, and following with songs like **Have Mercy**, "Jailhouse" (a reworking of the Wailers "Rude Boy"), **Them Never Love Poor Marcus**, **I Need A Roof**, and the brilliant **Right Time**, they established themselves as Jamaica's top vocal group.

Their success, locally and in the UK, spurred Virgin Records to release *The Right Time*, to universal acclaim. Containing most of the ground-breaking Channel One hits, the album ranks, with Spear's *Marcus Garvey*, Marley's *Natty Dread*, and the Congos' *Heart Of The Congos*, among the definitive vocal group albums of the 1970s. In 1976, the Diamonds toured the UK with U-Roy. Tracks recorded at the Lyceum Ballroom – scene of Bob Marley's triumphant concert the year before – have yet to appear on CD, but confirm the excitement they created.

The trio's next set for Virgin was the less well-received *Ice On Fire*, a collaboration with legendary New Orleans producer Allen Toussaint. They then returned to Channel One for the excellent Jamaican release *Stand Up To Your Judgement*, and two more Virgin albums, *Planet Earth* and *Deeper Roots*. While simultaneously releasing 45s on their own Bad Gong label, they next recorded for Joe Gibbs and Gussie Clarke. In early 1981, they hit again, with "Pass The Koochie" for Clarke, later covered by Musical Youth as "Pass the Dutchie".

The outstanding **Go Seek Your Rights** compilation contains all ten original tracks from *The Right Time*, plus six from *Planet Earth* and *Deeper Roots*. In the twenty years since these recordings were made, the Diamonds have managed to stay together, and they continue to tour regularly. The trio seem to be incapable of delivering substandard performances; they are simply one of the best harmony groups in the entire reggae field.

⊃ We almost chose **Heads of Government**, Penthouse, US, 1996

55

Jacob Miller

Who Say Jah No Dread

Greensleeves, 1992, UK

Recorded 1974–75. Jacob Miller (vocals). Mixed by King Tubby. Produced by
Augustus Pablo.

In 1968 Vocalist Al Campbell discovered Jacob Miller at the age of 13, singing in the schoolyard. Campbell, who sang for Studio One, took him straight down to Brentford Road, where young Jacob auditioned for Coxsone Dodd. Recognizing his talent immediately, Dodd recorded two songs. Only one, the plaintive rock steady ballad "Love Is A Message", was issued. The other – "My Girl Has Left Me" – used Larry Marshall's "Nanny Goat" rhythm; at this time, Dodd remained unconvinced of its new sound, and had yet to release Marshall's cut. Shortly thereafter, Jacob recorded "What More Can I Do" for Bunny Lee, written for him by the Cables.

Miller didn't record again until 1974, when he started to sing for innovative roots producer Augustus Pablo. **Who Say Jah No Dread** showcases six songs, and the corresponding dub versions, that they created during sessions in 1974 and 1975, and released as singles on Pablo's Rockers label. In 1976, Jacob went on to make local hits like "Tenement Yard" and the pro-herb "Tired Fe Lick Weed In A Bush", plus commercially oriented sides like "All Night 'Til Daylight", his 1976 Song Festival entry. Miller was then singing with Inner Circle, who released two albums on US Capitol in 1976 and 1977, and were a very strong live act.

From 1976 onwards, Inner Circle made a series of records for Tommy Cowan's Arab label, which like their later releases on

Top Ranking were very popular in Jamaica. Just how popular is demonstrated by the fact that Miller and Inner Circle were billed above Bob Marley and the Wailers for the famous 1978 Peace Concert in Kingston. That year, they signed with Island, releasing the commercially successful *Everything Is Great* album, which they followed up with *New Age Music* in 1979. Jacob also appeared memorably in the reggae movie *Rockers*. Everything looked set for the future, but the promise was not to be fulfilled. Returning from a recording session, Miller crashed his car into a tree and was killed instantly. His death (and the loss to reggae) was overshadowed by that of Bob Marley the following year, but Miller would surely have gone on to bigger and wider success.

Though Jacob's talent is abundantly evident on *Who Say Jah No Dread*, his is not the only light that shines. The rhythms, constructed by Pablo and musicians including the Barrett brothers, Leroy Sibbles, Robbie Shakespeare, Earl 'Chinna' Smith, as well as Pablo himself on keyboards and melodica, are superb. In addition, King Tubby was in absolute control at the mixing desk, creating astonishing, heart-stopping mixes that envelop the strong youthful tenor on the vocals, and wring every nuance from the supremely heavyweight rhythms on the dub versions. Miller's singing is strikingly mature for his age; he was only seventeen when he first recorded for Pablo, but he already had his own style, albeit inspired like so many others by Dennis Brown. Although in later years Miller was prone to an over-reliance on stutters and warbles to punctuate his vocals – in JA parlance, his "slurs" – such tendencies are barely noticeable here.

Of the three expressive love songs here, the best known is **Baby I Love You So**, the basis of the legendary dub **King Tubby Meets Rockers Uptown** (presented in a different mix from the usually anthologized version). Three equally vibrant roots tunes – **False Rasta**, **Who Say Jah No Dread**, and **Each One Teach One** qualify as some of the most deeply felt Rasta-themed music of the 1970s. This album truly does live up to its subtitle – "Classic Augustus Pablo Sessions".

⮞ We almost chose **Te Track...**, Greensleeves, UK, 1990

56

Sugar Minott

Black Roots

Black Roots, 1979, JA; Mango, 1990, US

Recorded 1979. Sugar Minott (vocals). Musicians include Noel Bailey (gtr), Tony Chin (gtr), Gladstone Anderson (bass), Ansel Collins (organ), Eric Clarke (drums), Junior Dan (bass), Steely Johnson (organ), Albert Malawi (drums), Noel Simms (pcn), Leroy 'Horsemouth' Wallace (drums). Produced by Sugar Minott.

Lincoln 'Sugar' Minott made three distinct contributions to the reggae scene during the first half of the 1980s: as an extremely individual and popular singer, as an accomplished producer, and as a very successful sound system operator. His career had started in the mid-1970s, when with Tony Tuff and Derrick Howard he formed a third of the African Brothers. Their commercial success was limited, but "Party Night", for Duke Thelwell, and the self-produced "Torturing" have become perennial 'revive' favourites in the UK, while Abyssinians-inspired outings like "Lead Us Father" and "Youths Of Today" are now seen as classics by roots followers.

After making the relatively weak single "No Cup No Brock" for Studio One, the African Brothers split up. Sugar himself, however, stayed at Brentford Road, where he showed an undeniable talent for fitting new lyrics over vintage rhythms. Unusually, his first significant impact came not through singles, but with his debut album, the accomplished *Live Loving*.

Minott then ventured away from Studio One – though Dodd was to continue releasing the material he had recorded there – to set up his own Black Roots and Youth Promotion labels. His first self-produced single, "Man Hungry", showed that he had graduated from the Brentford Road academy with honours, not merely developing his singing and songwriting, but also learning important studio skills as well. That impression was confirmed by the *Ghetto-Ology* album, on which it subsequently appeared.

The next self-produced set, **Black Roots**, was the first to appear on the label of that name. Though at least half a dozen Sugar Minott albums are essential for any reggae collection, none supersedes this 1979 classic, which catches the singer on the cusp of the roots and dancehall phases, and with total control over his music. Such was the buzz about his name at the time that Island/Mango released the album in the UK and US without any tampering to suit perceived crossover tastes. It's impossible to think of a more sympathetic production job. Sugar surrounded himself with the cream of Kingston's session musicians – including Studio One stalwarts Leroy 'Horsemouth' Wallace and Scully 'Zoot' Simms, Bingy Bunny and Eric 'Fish' Clarke from the Roots Radics, Twelve Tribes players Albert Malawi, Junior Dan and Michael Ras Star, and keyboards veterans Gladstone Anderson and Ansel Collins. For harmonies he was able to draw on the services of currently hot dancehall names like Don Carlos, Lacksley Castell and Ashanti Waugh. The result was an excellently performed, written and produced album, epitomizing all that was best in Jamaican music at the close of the 1970s.

A couple of tracks had already seen action as singles – **Hard Time Pressure**, which sold well as a UK twelve-inch, and the beautiful **River Jordan**. Fresh material, like **Black Roots** itself, **Oppression Oppression** (aka "Too Much Oppressors"), and **I'm Gonna Hold On**, was of a similar calibre. Except for the love song **Two Time Loser**, the focus throughout was on the runnings in the West Kingston ghettoes from which he'd emerged, and whose people he wanted to help with his Youth Promotion organization. For the 'lovers' side of Sugar, towards which his UK admirers increasingly led him, check his next album, *Roots Lovers*, but for cultural lyrics delivered in the most honeyed of tones, *Black Roots* is the first-choice Sugar Minott.

➲ We almost chose **Showcase**, Heartbeat, US/UK, 1992

57

Jackie Mittoo

Tribute to Jackie Mittoo

Heartbeat, 1995, US/UK

Recorded 1965–69. Jackie Mittoo (organ), with the Soul Brothers, the Soul Vendors, and the Sound Dimension. Produced by Coxsone Dodd.

Quite simply, Jackie Mittoo was the most important reggae musician of all time. Without his contribution, modern reggae is unimaginable. Born Donat Roy Mittoo on March 3, 1948, he was taught to play the piano by his grandmother from the age of four. Like another Jamaican musical prodigy, the jazz pianist Monty Alexander, Jackie began his professional career after school hours. He would also cut lessons altogether to make sessions at Federal Studio. By 1961, Mittoo was playing piano in bands like the Rivals. A couple of years later, having been a member of the Sheiks and Cavaliers Combo, he came to the attention of Coxsone Dodd, who recognized his precocious abilities and asked him to lead sessions at Studio One.

So it was that Jackie became a founder member of the Skatalites, launching an association that produced much of Jamaica's greatest music. A member of all Coxsone's major studio bands – the Soul Brothers, the Soul Vendors, and the Sound Dimension – he played on thousands of sides. As well as arranging for, and backing, all the leading artists, he cut many singles under his own name. Coxsone also released a series of albums of his Hammond B-3 organ instrumentals – a blend of such US artists as Booker T and Jimmy Smith over reggae rhythms.

In the process of making this vast body of music, Mittoo – and protegés like bassist Leroy Sibbles of the Heptones – laid the foundation for modern reggae. The rhythms he and the Studio One musicians created during the late 1960s have been copied ever since. They were the basis from which Bunny Lee, Augustus Pablo, and Sly Dunbar, fashioned much of their mid-1970s output, which led in turn to the "dancehall" phenomenon of the late 1970s and early 1980s. Even the arrival of digital recording, sampling and other technical innovations has not diminished the reliance – some might say over-reliance – on the corpus created thirty years ago by Jackie and his colleagues.

By the mid-1970s, Mittoo was in Toronto, running the Stine-Jac label with Jerry Jackson. Bunny Lee also teamed him with Sly and Robbie for a series of stunning albums, while in the mid-1980s he worked with Sugar Minott and was director for the pop-reggae group Musical Youth. In the years preceding his tragically early death from cancer in December 1990, he worked with producers like Kenneth 'Skengdon' Black in Miami and Lloyd 'Bullwackie' Barnes in the Bronx.

Even though most of its 31 tracks are new to album, the splendid two-CD compilation **Tribute to Jackie Mittoo** does full credit to Jackie's crucial significance, with an essay by Skatalites historian Brian Keyo, rare photos, and reminiscences from associates. Although it includes a couple of vocals – Alton Ellis' **Blackman's Pride** and Jackie's own **Got My Boogaloo** – the focus is on brilliant instrumental workouts. Among funky originals are **Ghetto Organ**, **Hot Tamale**, **Memphis Groove**, and **Some Kind Of Memphis**. Other cuts, like **Nature Boy** with Count Ossie's drummers, or **Mission Impossible**, a jumping reggae take on "Old Man River", offer jazzy variations on standards. New explorations of classic songs, such as the Righteous Flames' "I Was Born To Love You" (**Gold Streak**) or the Heptones' "Fatty Fatty" (**Gold Mine**), stand alongside better-known hits like **West Of The Sun**, featuring Ernest Ranglin, and **Drum Song**. Throughout the set, Mittoo's musicality and soulfulness shine brightly, underlining what a loss his death was. Reggae organ, it would seem, starts and ends here.

⮕ We almost chose **Evening Time**, Studio One, US, 1996

58

Harry Mudie

Meets King Tubby In Dub Conference Vol 1

Moodisc, 1976, US

Recorded 1976. Engineered by King Tubby. Produced by Harry Mudie.

Harry Mudie was definitely a producer with his own ideas, as was reflected in the distinctive range of artists and material with which he chose to work. In the early '60s, Mudie was among the first to record with legendary Rasta drummer Count Ossie. When the reggae age dawned in 1968, he was making classics at Studio One like the Ebony Sisters' "Let Me Tell You Boy", and Dennis Walks' "The Drifter" and "Heart Don't Leap". All three have turned out to rank among the most enduring rhythms in dancehall history.

Mudie also cut plenty of instrumentals, most notably with trumpeter Jo Jo Bennett, vibes player Lennie Hibbert, and saxophonist Carl 'Cannonball' Bryan. During the 1970s, he produced excellent easy-listening reggae with pianist Gladstone Anderson and saxophonist Ossie Scott, as well as some of John Holt's best work. In addition, he discovered the accomplished vocalist Bunny Maloney, cutting two albums with him in the late 1970s that still sound good today. These days, Mudie seems content to reissue his catalogue from his base in Miami, while occasionally testing out artists on his classic rhythms. Thus Horace Andy and Tinga Stewart both cut 1980s songs on the classic late-1960s Mudie rhythms mentioned above, as did deejays like the innovative late Nicodemus and the lesser-known Johnny Cool.

Dub Conference Volume 1 was mixed in 1976, as the vogue for dub albums was really starting to take off. Its ten tracks feature deconstructions by King Tubby of several of Mudie's finest rhythms. Working on a four-track Luntz mixing desk from the former kitchen of his house at 18 Dromilly Avenue, Waterhouse, Tubby had by this time got dub down to a fine art. Standout cuts include scintillating dub versions of Dennis Walks' cover of Sweet Sensation's pop-soul hit "Sad Sweet Dreamer" (**Dub Conference** itself), Ossie Scott's version of US sax star Grover Washington's "Lorna's Dance" and "Mr Magic" (**Full Dose of Dub** and **Heavy Duty Dub**), John Holt's "Gone Is The Love" (**Dub With A Difference**), Jo Jo Bennett's "Leaving Rome" (**Roman Dub**), and Louisa Marks' "Caught You In A Lie" (**Caught You Dubbing**).

Unlike the more extrovert dancehall style Tubby used on dubs for Bunny Lee and other producers, these are some of his subtlest mixes, designed to wring out every intricacy of Mudie's classy arrangements. King Tubby was a connoisseur of many styles of music, including jazz. He tailored his style to fit that of the music he mixed, but it is still unmistakably his hand manipulating the equalization, high-pass filter, reverb and delay. All these effects – the sound Bunny Lee called "Doctor Satan's echo chamber" – are in evidence throughout *Dub Conference*.

Tubby customized every component of his studio hardware himself. Thus a standard Fisher reverb unit would become a Tubby's reverb, once the engineer had altered it in line with local requirements and his own exacting standards. His dub mixes often completely transformed the "feel" of a tune. "Dub With A Difference", for example, truly lives up to its title. John Holt's original ballad is changed into an eerie mix of rhythm and haunting strings, the latter processed through a phasing effect which makes the orchestra sound as if it's beamed in from some far-distant radio station.

The *Dub Conference* series includes two more superb volumes. The second set is drawn from the same period as the first, while the third displays Tubby at work on rhythms from the late 1970s. All these provide a stunning introduction to the sound, simultaneously had and classy, of one of the most under-rated producers in Jamaican music.

➲ We almost chose **Dub Conference Vol 2**, Moodisc, US, 1997

59

Johnny Osbourne

Truths and Rights

Studio One, 1980, JA; Heartbeat, 1992, US

Recorded 1979. Johnny Osbourne (vocals). Produced by Coxsone Dodd.

Though his career in music goes back to the late 1960s, few singers so personify the dancehall era as Johnny Osbourne. Like his main rival of the early '80s, Frankie Paul, he possessed the knack of being able to sing over any rhythm that was hot in the dance. Though Johnny's debut record, "All I Have Is Love" with a group called the Wildcats, was recorded at Studio One, his first Jamaican hit, "Come Back Darling", was cut for Winston Riley. The album that followed included the roots classic "Purify Your Heart" and the marvellous "Warrior", which was successfully revived by both Bunny Wailer and Marcia Griffiths in the 1990s. After that, Johnny went to Canada, where he recorded with the Ishan People outfit.

Sustained success only came upon his return to Jamaica in 1979, starting with three thoughtful singles for Dodd – "Jealousy, Heartache and Pain", "Forgive Them", and "Love is Here To Stay". Johnny made just one album for Studio One, **Truths and Rights**, before he embarked upon the usual label hopping, yielding major Jamaican hits for Henry 'Junjo' Lawes ("Ice Cream Love"), Jimbo ("Yo-Yo"), Channel One ("Lend Me Your Chopper"), Linval Thompson ("Back Off"), and Prince Jammy ("Water Pumping"). The pace did eventually slow down, but the digital age still saw such outstanding singles as "Budy Bye", "Rewind", and "In Your Area" for Jammy, "Mother Africa" for Hugh 'Redman' James, "Good Time Rock" for Bobby Digital,

"Salute the Don" for Steely & Clevie, and "Hill & Gully" for George Phang.

In 1978, Sugar Minott's ground-breaking debut set for Studio One, *Live Loving*, showed that it was possible to sing fresh lyrics over vintage rhythms and have them fit just as well as the originals. *Truths and Rights*, released a couple of years later, followed much the same formula with comparable success. In fact, Johnny never left his Studio One heritage completely behind; the dancehall era to which he made such a major contribution was largely based on reworkings of classic rock steady or early reggae bass lines that began life at Brentford Road. However, Johnny obviously spent a little longer on the lyrics when he was recording *Truths and Rights*, and that made the difference.

Another advantage it had over many of the dancehall sets that were to come was its avoidance of over-familiar rhythms. Only the Soul Vendors' "Swing Easy" – employed for **Can't Buy Love** – was already a dancehall favourite. **Truths and Rights** itself, with its heartfelt warnings about sudden destruction, was supported by Al Campbell's "Take A Ride" – a tune appreciated by the cognoscenti, but never a Jamaican hit. Similarly, **We Need Love**, possibly the album's most memorable track, utilizes Otis Gayle's "I Get Around" – again, a cult favourite only. As well as employing the rhythm of the Chosen Few's "Don't Break Your Promise", **Jah Promise** was obviously influenced by the lyric of the original, but it still manages to sound fresh – partly because despite being one of the group's best-known tunes, it had hardly been versioned.

Sing Jah Stylee, employing Alexander Henry's "Please Be True" rhythm, is a lot nearer to the pure dancehall mood of Johnny's subsequent work. The lyrics describe him dancing with a girl, who tells him: "Johnny, you a really groovy star / She says my lyrics real crucial / Me even sing Christmas carol." As, indeed, Johnny Osbourne – or any self-respecting dancehall performer – could. For the more serious side of his talent, check the rest of the tracks on *Truths and Rights*.

➲ We almost chose **Nightfall Showcase**, Majestic Reggae, Holland, 1997

60

Count Ossie

Remembering Count Ossie

Moodisc, 1996, US

Recorded 1960–63. Count Ossie (drums), with the Wareikas (pcn), Bobby 'Big Bra' Gaynair (tenor sax), and Rico Rodriguez (trombone). Produced by Harry A. Mudie.

Subtitled "A Rasta Reggae Legend", the nineteen-track **Remembering Count Ossie** CD compiles all the music made by legendary drummer Count Ossie for producer Harry Mudie during the early 1960s. Born in 1926, Oswald Williams pioneered the use of Rasta drumming in Jamaican music. He first came into contact with the technique in the shanty towns of Kingston in the late 1940s. The followers of Leonard Howell, a founding father of modern Rasta, had recently moved to the Kingston ghettoes after Howell's Pinnacle settlement outside Spanish Town was closed down by the colonial state forces. Having adopted the African-derived 'burru' drumming style to accompany their songs of praise, they were known as the burru people.

Many musicians and singers visited Rasta camps in and around Kingston during the 1950s, to reason with the elders and smoke the herb chalice. Among those who frequented Ossie's camp were the jazz-schooled instrumentalists who formed the core of the Skatalites, including trombonist Don Drummond, trumpeter Dizzy Moore, and saxophonists Roland Alphonso and Tommy McCook.

Norman C. Weinstein devotes a chapter in his book *A Night In Tunisia: Imaginings Of Africa In Jazz* to Count Ossie, discussing two albums recorded in the first half of the 1970s, the triple set

Grounation and the follow-up *Tales Of Mozambique*. He argues convincingly that Ossie's large drum-dominated aggregations of this period made a significant contribution to the body of diasporic music, recorded in the Americas, that consciously looks to Africa for its inspiration.

Count Ossie's group was invited to the 1974 Newport Jazz Festival by Duke Ellington and Randy Weston, but his career in recorded music went back to 1960, when his Afro-Combo backed the Folkes Brothers on "Oh Carolina" for Prince Buster. In search of a new, more 'Jamaican' sound, Buster had gone to the Rasta camp at Warricka Hill on the outskirts of Kingston to request Ossie's participation on a session. Ossie and his drummers played for Coxsone around the same time, but most of their recording was for the Spanish Town producer Harry A. Mudie.

Those sessions, all collected on this excellent CD, present us with an early instance of the African penetration, in the form of Ossie's drummers, of Jamaican popular music, as represented by outstanding players like trombonist Emanuel Rico Rodriguez and saxist Bobby Gaynair. They deliver several excellent jazz-styled solos, and producer Mudie has also added sound effects to certain tracks, which don't detract from the overall quality of the music. On those sides, the African elements are not fully absorbed, but the point is made. The Rasta chanting style is fully manifested on the songs **So Long The Negus Call You**, **One Bright Morning**, and **Babylon Gone**; on other selections, the boogie-based US-style Jamaican instrumental r'n'b is augmented with the full Rasta drum sound of funde, akete and repeater.

The next development in Jamaican music, ska, drew on many other styles for inspiration, but its definitive rhythmic emphasis was similarly Afro-Jamaican. Perhaps most importantly, from here on in, Rasta themes were to feature ever more prominently. Ossie himself died in a traffic accident in 1976, but his personal legacy is extended in the work of the Mystic Revelation Of Rastafari, and in his "Kette Drum" rhythm, which recently resurfaced in the Jamaican dancehall hits of producer Bobby Digital.

➲ We almost chose **Ras Michael: Rastafari**, Greensleeves, UK, 1992

61

Augustus Pablo

King Tubby Meets The Rockers Uptown

Rockers/Jetstar, 1998, UK/JA

Recorded 1972–75. Augustus Pablo (kbds), Robbie Shakespeare, Aston 'Family Man' Barrett (bass), Carlton Barrett (drums), Earl 'Chinna' Smith (gtr), and others. King Tubby (dub mixes). Produced by Augustus Pablo.

If you had to pick just one album to represent dub, **King Tubby Meets The Rockers Uptown** is the disc. The title really says it all: the collaboration between the premier engineer and the top roots producer of the mid-'70s resulted in definitive King Tubby interpretations of some of Pablo's deepest rhythms. It also demonstrated conclusively that a studio engineer could be considered as creative as the singers, musicians and visionary producer who made the music.

A dub is essentially a remix. In the hands of an engineer as good as King Tubby (1941–1989) it became an artform, and an incredibly popular one. From the 1970s on, Tubby cut dubs for all the top sound systems and producers. The impact of his pioneering efforts has since resounded far beyond its birthplace in the dancehall and it shows no sign of diminishing.

Back in 1972, at the time of this recording, King Tubby was based in the Waterhouse ghetto, and was the acknowledged ruler of the sound system world. Pablo (1953–1999), a scion of the more 'uptown' Swaby family, was aged just 19 but had begun producing himself and already knew the sound he was seeking: a minor chord-based 'Far East' sound. This is what came to fruition on *King Tubby Meets The Rockers Uptown* and it was a major component in the whole roots sound of the '70s, forged along with others of similar spiritual temperament, like Yabby You.

For this ground-breaking disc, Pablo assembled a brilliant cast: the Upsetters/Wailers drum and bass duo of Aston 'Family Man' Barrett and brother Carlton, guitarist Earl 'Chinna' Smith, horns-men Richard 'Dirty Harry' Hall, Bobby Ellis, Vin Gordon and bassist Robbie Shakespeare. All sessions were recorded by the engineer Errol 'ET' Thompson at Randy's studio on North Parade. Pablo then took the tapes to King Tubby for mixing. He initially released instrumental, deejay and vocal cuts as 7-inch 45s on his Hot Stuff, Rockers and Pablo International labels, between 1972 and 75, but as the vogue for dub albums exploded in 1976, Pablo compiled twelve of his b-side dubs to make this set.

The centrepiece of the album is **King Tubby Meets The Rockers Uptown**, a killer dub version of Jacob Miller's vocal "Baby I Love You So" which almost single-handedly defined dub for a non-Jamaican audience when it was released as a single by Island Records (UK) in 1975; it also appeared on the company's massive-selling *This Is Reggae Music* sampler. Using his custom sliders, Tubby eases Miller's voice in and out of the mix, adding stabs of guitar and melodica. Carlton Barrett's explosive snare fills further serve to punctuate the elastic rhythm, which was first cut for producer Herman Chin Loy's 1973 album *Aquarius Dub*. Similarly, **Frozen Dub** propelled the Heptones on a recut of their Studio One classic "Love Won't Come Easy".

Hopefully someone, some day, will undertake to present this crucial set in all its glory, with alternate mixes. This CD reissue could do with better remastering and more care. Unaccountably, the exclamation "Lion!" is missing from the beginning of the album's opener, **Keep On Dubbing**. Oddly, too, the record's last track is not actually listed on the CD, though it's there on the disc: it's Pablo's take on the Abyssinians' classic anthem **Satta Massagana**, given a beautifully understated mix by Tubby. But quibbles aside, this really is an essential essential – and, especially given that *Blackboard Jungle*, Tubby's epic collaboration with Scratch, continues to be poorly reissued, it is the first of all dub CDs to acquire for any collection.

➦ Nothing compares

62

Augustus Pablo

Original Rockers

Greensleeves, 1987, UK

Recorded 1972–75. Augustus Pablo (melodica, kbds). Musicians include Aston 'Family Man' Barrett (bass), Earl 'Chinna' Smith (gtr), Carlton Barrett (drums), Bobby Ellis (trmpt), Don D Junior (trmbne), Richard "Dirty Harry" Hall (sax). Mixed by Philip Smart, King Tubby and Prince Jammy. Produced by Augustus Pablo.

Original Rockers may be a very short CD – its ten tracks run just over 29 minutes – but the music that it contains is quite outstanding. First issued on vinyl in 1979, it brings together rare sides that appeared as 7-inch singles on Pablo's own labels between 1972 and 1975; to obtain original first pressings now would probably cost in excess of £500.

Born Horace Swaby in Kingston (1953–1999), Augustus Pablo made his debut on a series of singles for Herman Chin Loy's Aquarius label in 1969 and 1970. Cuts like the moody minor-key "East Of The River Nile" provided clues to his future direction. He joined up with producer Clive Chin (formerly Pablo's fellow pupil at Kingston College), cutting 1972's big hit "Java" as a melodica instrumental when the vocalist scheduled to sing on the rhythm couldn't make the session.

Pablo then started his own labels, Hot Stuff and Rockers, the latter named after the sound system owned by his brother Garth. His debut album, *This Is Augustus Pablo* in 1973, was issued by Clive Chin and mixed by Errol 'ET' Thompson, but from late 1972 onwards, all Pablo's own tunes were recorded at Dynamic (later Channel One), and mixed at King Tubby's. Pablo's timing was perfect; Tubby was just establishing his kingdom of dub in his kitchen at 18 Dromilly Avenue, Waterhouse. Pablo played all the keyboards – organ, piano, clavinet, glockenspiel and his famous melodica – and used the Wailers' rhythm section of 'Family Man' Barrett on bass and his brother Carlton on drums.

Over their foundation, Earl 'Chinna' Smith played guitar, with horns by 'Dirty Harry' Hall, Vin Gordon, and Bobby Ellis. Whether Pablo originals or Studio One recuts, the instrumentals they made share their minor key and evocative mood with the ska and rock steady models that were their inspiration. A couple of tracks here feature deejaying, including a version of the Heptones' classic "Love Won't Come Easy" (**Rockers Dub**), on which Pablo and Paul K supply the interjections, and a great early Dillinger called **Brace A Boy**, plus the b-side for good measure – a glockenspiel version known as **AP Special**. There are two excellent out-and-out dubs, full of the Tubby style – dramatic horns sprayed through long delay, cavernous reverb, clattering guitar chops; **Jah Dread**, a different mix of Jacob Miller's "Who Say Jah No Dread", and **Park Lane Special**, the original b-side dub to Hugh Mundell's "Africa Must Be Free". Instrumentals include **Thunderclap**, a brooding clavinet rendition, one-finger style, of the "Ain't No Sunshine" rhythm also used by Dr Alimantado on "Best Dressed Chicken In Town".

Cassava Piece is named after a lane in Kingston; it's the melodica version of the rhythm later used for Jacob Miller's epic "Baby I Love You So" / "King Tubby Mets The Rockers Uptown". The cut called **Tubby's Dub Song** here is actually the other side of the record, "Pablo's Theme Song", another melodica instrumental; the correct dub cut has since been reissued by Pressure Sounds.

If melodica instrumentals don't sound very enticing, prepare to be surprised. Between 1972 and 1977, Augustus Pablo was at his best; aided by some barbwire-taut rhythms and supremely dynamic mixes, Pablo blew his bittersweet melodies through his little Hohner keyboard, making it sing the songs of King Alpha, and thereby created a string of minor masterpieces.

➲ We almost chose **Authentic Golden Melodies**, Rockers/Jetstar, UK, 1998

63

Frankie Paul

Sara

Jammy's, 1987, JA; Fatman, 1997, UK

Recorded 1987. Frankie Paul (vocals). Musicians include Danny Browne (kbds),
Clevie Browne (drums, kbds), Steely Johnson (bass, kbds). Produced by King
Jammy.

The most exciting – and prolific –
singer to appear during the
dancehall phase of the early 1980s
was Frankie Paul. Born virtually
blind, as Paul Blake, in Kingston
in 1965, his early inspiration was
the American soul star Stevie
Wonder, who visited the special
school that he attended. The
other obvious influence on the
records that established him in
1982 and 1983 was Dennis Brown. But if, as these models sug-
gest, Paul was a 'real' singer in the traditional sense, he also possessed the important ability endlessly to put new lyrics to the
tried and tested rhythms that were then running Kingston's
dancehalls. Another factor that made him the dancehall singer
par excellence was his diligence in applying his talent towards
cutting hits for every producer on the island. Those that he made
for Channel One, Winston Riley, Henry 'Junjo' Lawes and
George Phang were most emphatic in declaring the arrival of an
enduring star.

While several of Paul's contemporaries failed to adapt to the
next major upset in the music, the shift to digital rhythms in
1985, he obviously experienced no difficulties. He returned to
Winston Riley for more hits, as well as successfully recording for
producers such as Jack Scorpio, Redman, Steely and Clevie,
Tommy Cowan and, for his most consistent run, King Jammy.

The man born Lloyd James had not only been the producer and sound system man who initiated computerized rhythms with Wayne Smith's "Under Me Sleng Teng" in 1985, but he continued effortlessly to rule the dancehall for the rest of the decade. The sheer number of quality rhythms that emerged from his studio at 38 St Lucia Road during this period was staggering, and their very real musical values made them ideal for the still highly prolific Paul. Almost all the Frankie Paul singles that appeared on Jammy's label were worth picking up, and at least three of his albums deserve a place in any reggae collection. **Sara**, nonetheless, which first appeared in 1987, remains the place to start. The title track itself, Sara, had been massive not only in Jamaica, but in all the reggae capitals of the world. The subsequent Jammy-produced album proceeded to sell almost as if it were a single.

The reasons are not hard to find. Though the original vinyl release held only nine tracks, each featured Paul singing his heart out over one of Jammy's strongest rhythms, and could easily have been a hit. As it was, only one other track, I Know the Score, was released as a single. A similarly heartfelt love song, employing an exceptional Steely and Clevie reworking of the Studio One chestnut "Throw Me Corn", it almost repeated the success of "Sara", and arguably now sounds even stronger. Even a title as banal as Kissing In the Dark becomes transformed into something of substance thanks not only to the crisp digital rhythm, but the sheer exuberance the young Frankie brings to a far stronger lyric than might be expected.

Away from affairs of the heart, FP, as he's known in his frequent self-references, tackles the expected topics – dancehall runnings, rudeboy business, self-celebration, and the odd cultural deliberation. The CD adds six tracks to the original nine, including the exquisite Didn't Mean To Turn You On, which was listed on the LP cover but did not actually show up on the record, and another five of a similar calibre. Frankie Paul in the '80s really should have had major crossover success.

⮑ We almost chose **Pass The Tu-Shun-Peng...**, Greensleeves, UK, 1985

64

Lee Perry

Arkology

Island Jamaica, 1997, UK

Recorded 1974–79. Produced by Lee Perry. Artists include The Upsetters, Max Romeo, the Heptones, the Congos, the Meditations, Junior Murvin, Mikey Dread, Errol Walker, Dr Alimantado, Augustus Pablo, Keith Rowe, George Faith.

The diminutive singer and producer Lee 'Scratch' Perry – who was born Rainford Hugh Perry in 1936, in Hanover, Jamaica – made his initial impact performing at Studio One in the ska era. Having then run sessions for Joe Gibbs, he went on to produce for himself, creating a powerful initial impact with innovative work from the Wailers, as well as singers like Junior Byles, Leo Graham and Max Romeo, and an impressive early dub set, *Blackboard Jungle*. By 1974, he had built his own Black Ark studio behind his home in Washington Gardens, and was busy developing the distinctive sound with which he's most associated. This involved using equipment like an Echoplex reverb unit and Mutron Phaser to create a dense 'underwater' ambience. Like so much cutting-edge reggae, it exemplified the Jamaican approach to making maximum demands of minimal resources. Sound textures that were in any case unique were further developed through working with a Teac four-track recorder, which meant the dumping of completed tracks onto one track. The subsequent loss of 'sound quality' in the normal sense then contributed to the incomparable feel of Scratch's music.

The sheer quantity of Black Ark music that's now easily available can be daunting to the newcomer. However, taking into account both sound quality and actual track selection, the recommended starting point must be the triple-CD, 52-track **Arkology** set, complete with informative booklet. For the more seasoned Upsetter collector with every 7- and 12-inch single, it also offers fifteen previously unreleased tracks. When it comes to the best-known hits, these are invariably followed by further chapter and version. Thus the most famous single ever to emerge from the studio, Junior Murvin's **Police and Thieves**, is presented not just with its dub, but as part of a five-track suite that also includes Glen DaCosta's saxophone cut, Jah Lloyd's deejay version and a further voicing from the singer, **Bad Weed**. Similarly, a hitherto unreleased take of the Heptones classic **Sufferer's Time** leads into an extended mix of the dub and a Junior Dread toast, while Scratch's own **Dreadlocks In Moonlight** comes in tandem with the Mikey Dread version. Very often, the twelve-inch mix of a track is used, which works to particularly striking effect on Max Romeo's story of the gambler **Norman**; that's Jah Lloyd playing the domino, incidentally.

The often under-celebrated Romeo stands as a star of the set, also heard at his most memorable on the popular **War In A Babylon**, **One Step Forward**, and **Chase the Devil**. The Meditations, who provided harmonies for many Black Ark sessions, come into their own on three arresting roots tunes, while Devon Irons' very scarce **Ketch Vampire** will fill a gap in many a collection, as will Augustus Pablo's **Vibrate On**, which has his melodica sounding totally at home in the smoky atmosphere of the Black Ark. To show that the dense studio sound could just as successfully be applied to romantic concerns there's George Faith's **To Be A Lover** and Keith Rowe's **Groovy Situation**.

Despite all the obvious talent of the singers, deejays and musicians involved, there's no denying the principal organizing consciousness throughout. Whether a tirade against Babylon or a soul-inflected ballad, a classic example of group-vocal artistry or a wild dubonic adventure, all the tracks are part of a voyage to the outer limits of sound, piloted by the Upsetter, aka Scratch, aka the Dub Organizer.

➲ We almost chose **Produced and Directed...**, Pressure Sounds, UK, 1998

65

Lee Perry

Super Ape

Upsetter/Island, 1976, JA/UK

Recorded 1976. Musicians include Prince Jazzbo (vocals), Max Romeo (vocals), the Heptones (vocals), Boris Gardiner (bass), Mikey 'Boo' Richards (drums), Earl 'Chinna' Smith (gtr), Keith Sterling (pno), Bobby Ellis (trumpet), Herman Marquis (sax), Richard 'Dirty Harry' Hall (sax), Vin Gordon (tbne). Produced by Lee Perry.

According to Max Romeo, the sound of Black Ark – saturated in reverb, delay, and tape hiss – was not apparent until Lee Perry, the self-styled 'dub shepherd', was at the controls. While the Teac four-track recorders and Echoplex delay unit are by today's standards primitive, in Perry's hands they were instruments of magic, conjuring a raw, organic naturality into the music that hovers over **Super Ape** with an almost tangible presence. Originally credited to the Upsetters when released as *Scratch The Super Ape* in Jamaica in early 1976, it shows Perry in full control of the studio he had built during 1973 and 1974. His first recordings there were fairly basic, although Junior Byles' poignant "Curly Locks" was a big hit, but a deal with Island UK resulted in outboard acquisitions for the mixing board. Scratch produced excellent sets by Max Romeo, the Heptones, George Faith, Junior Murvin and Jah Lloyd for the label, and Bob Marley cut some of his best tunes there, too, towards the end of his career.

Super Ape is really an instrumental album with dub manipulation; occasionally, refrains and snatches of vocal appear, by the Heptones, Prince Jazzbo, James Brown, and Perry himself. On his two subsequent solo albums from Black Ark – *Return Of The*

Super Ape and *Roast Fish and Cornbread* – he featured himself more fully, but here he restricts his vocal contribution to the odd verse, delivered in his half-sung, half-spoken deejay style. The album is all the better for it; the focus is thus on the magnificent music, played by some of the best players of the day; Boris Gardiner, Mikey Richards, Earl Smith and Keith Sterling played rhythm, while Bobby Ellis, Herman Marquis, Richard Hall and Vin Gordon executed the full horn charts. Moreover, despite the lack of Perry vocals, the producer's 'voice' really does emerge, perhaps even more strongly with hindsight, given Perry's persona as a performer since he left Jamaica in the early 1980s.

Super Ape itself is a perfect illustration of Perry's authorial role. Though he uses artists and musicians to fashion the elements he then juggles in the mix, the vision and sentiments are unmistakeably his. The Heptones introduce the piece with the refrain "This is the ape man, trodding through creation, step with I-man", repeated at intervals throughout the song, in which flute (by Egbert Evans) and whistles also feature strongly and mysteriously; it finally fades with Prince Jazzbo intoning "I no deal with war" through a deep delay. This gives way seamlessly into an alternate version of Jazzbo's Croaking Lizard, on which Scratch plays superbly with the deejay's voice throughout. Dub Along has the Blue Bells girl group expressing the producer's sentiments ("Follow I, Follow I . . . Dub with I, Dub with I") over a stately drum, bass and electric piano rhythm.

A couple of tracks have turned up elsewhere; the atmospheric Zion Blood and Black Vest were both used by Max Romeo, and Dread Lion was also deejayed by Prince Jazzbo ("Natty Pass Through Rome"). What's here known as Underground Root was used for a celebrated dubplate played by the champion UK sound of the 1970s, called "From Creation" by Clive Hylton. The remaining tunes are exclusive to *Super Ape*, which together with the Congos' *Heart Of The Congos* represents the fullest single-album realization of the producer's unique vision.

➲ We almost chose **Voodooism**, Pressure Sounds, UK, 1996

66

Jimmy Radway/Various Artists

Keep the Pressure Down

Fe Me Time, 1999, UK

Recorded 1972–75. Artists include Scatty Bell, Big Youth, Errol Dunkley, Augustus Pablo, Leroy Smart, Desmond Young. Produced by Jimmy Radway.

The roots explosion of the 1970s brought not just a great influx of fresh young singers and deejays into the Kingston recording studios, but the arrival of a large number of exciting new producers. Many operated with the minimum of financial backing, and each was compelled to make his mark with a distinctive sound of his own – even if most were using permutations of the same pool of seasoned session musicians. Some important innovators like Vivian Jackson and Augustus Pablo have since found the broad audience they always deserved, while others such as the quirky Glen Brown have at least been the subject of intelligently compiled and annotated compilations. Foremost among the great originators who up to now have been almost totally ignored outside of the reggae cognoscenti has been Jimmy Radway, whose finest work has now been gathered on **Keep The Pressure Down**.

Born in Kingston in 1947, this incredibly consistent – if not particularly prolific – producer recorded a series of seminal singles from talented singers Errol Dunkley, Leroy Smart, Hortense Ellis, Desmond Young, and the more obscure Scatty Bell, as well as the most popular deejays of the day, Big Youth and I-Roy. A former upholsterer, his strongest rhythms were also reconstructed for an awesome dub set mixed by Errol 'ET' Thompson that appeared in a very limited press on Pete Weston's Micron imprint, and has been reissued a couple of times by European labels, but never with the packaging and promotion it warrants.

The initial production on Radway's Fe Mi Time label was also his first hit – Errol Dunkley's much-versioned **Black Cinderella** reached the top spot on the Jamaican charts in early 1972. Before January was over, it was treated to cuts from Big Youth, fresh from the Lord Tippertone sound system, and the melodica player Augustus Pablo. Later, I-Roy's brilliant "Sound Education" toast appeared on the same rhythm. Thanks to the informative liner notes here, we now learn that the original song was inspired by a girl Radway knew, both of whose sisters were prostitutes, but who was determined to resist that way of life.

The nagging trombone figure that contributed so much to the rhythm's popularity was from Vin Gordon. Distinctive horn arrangements – usually involving Bobby Ellis on trumpet and Richard 'Dirty Harry' Hall on tenor sax – were a distinguishing characteristic of many Jimmy Radway productions. The memorable organ-dominated rhythm for Radway's other Dunkley track, the impassioned **Keep the Pressure Down**, was never as popular, but sounds just as magnificent, and remains long overdue for other producers to revive. The incisive sufferer's lyrics were again from the pen of Radway, confirming his truly creative approach. Big Youth is also in fine form on **Tribulation**. One of his scarcest outings, it appeared previously only on a blank-label pressing of the rhythm's first cut, Hortense Ellis' **Hell and Sorrow**.

The trio of titles from the gritty-voiced Leroy Smart – **Mother Liza**, **Mirror Mirror**, and **Happiness Is My Desire** – arguably amount to his greatest work, mainly thanks to Radway's superior lyrics. A pity they didn't make an entire album together. Desmond Young's popular **Warning** and Scatty Bell's **Black I Am** were two of 1975's greatest roots records, and again it can only be regretted that Radway didn't record more with either. Unfortunately, he eventually tired of the bear pit of the Kingston recording scene and quietly backed away.

⮞ We almost chose **Randy's: 17 North Parade**, Pressure Sounds, UK, 1997

Ernest Ranglin

Sounds and Power

Studio One, 1996, US

Recorded 1968–95. Ernest Ranglin (gtr), plus the Soul Vendors and the Sound Dimension, with Monty Alexander (melodica), Cedric Brooks (sax), Karl Bryan (sax), Vin Gordon (trombone), David Madden (trumpet), Jackie Mittoo (kbds). Produced by Coxsone Dodd.

An internationally respected jazz guitarist for over three decades, Ernest Ranglin was also one of the foundation musicians of reggae. Born in 1932 in Manchester, Jamaica, Ranglin was playing the live circuit in popular swing bands, like those of Eric Deans and Val Bennett, while he was still a teenager. By the late 1950s, he had joined up with musicians such as trombonists Rico Rodriguez and Don Drummond, tenor saxophonist Roland Alphonso, and trumpeters Oswald 'Baba' Brooks and Johnny 'Dizzy' Moore, to play the local variations of American r'n'b being recorded by Duke Reid. During the same period, Ranglin also sat in with Clue J and the Blues Blasters, the main session band for the Duke's arch rival Clement "Sir Coxsone" Dodd. He considers what they were playing then to be the first ska records. Certainly those kind of sessions led directly to Jamaica's declaration of musical independence in the early years of the 1960s, and the formation of the prolific Skatalites, with whom Ranglin sometimes recorded.

With the advent of the romanticism and heavy bass lines of rock steady in 1966, Ranglin again played a key role, sometimes supervising sessions at Duke Reid's Treasure Isle studio. Even during the 1970s, he still took breaks from jazz gigging to play for the island's top producers, and recorded the laidback instrumental masterpiece "Surfing" for Clement Dodd.

In recent years, due perhaps to an overdue recognition of Jamaica's contribution to jazz, Ranglin has taken on a much higher profile. Well-received albums have appeared on the Island Jamaica Jazz, Palm Pictures, Grove Music and Kariang labels. Not to be outdone, Clement Dodd at last got around in 1996 to issuing the first album from Jamaica's most accomplished guitarist on Studio One. **Sounds and Power** was very much in the great tradition of classic Studio One instrumental albums, stretching back to Jackie Mittoo's efforts in the late 1960s and early 1970s. Jackie's 1970 set *Macka Fat* was the template for equally strong sets from Roland Alphonso and fellow saxophonist Cedric Brooks, as well as Pablove Black on various keyboard instruments. The formula could not have been simpler, or the results more satisfying: already proven rhythms were dusted off, and the featured musician would coolly extemporize over them.

In common with all these albums, the feel of Ranglin's set is very relaxed, as though his main concern is simply to enjoy himself over some very familiar rhythm tracks. On the Eternals' late 1960s hit "Stars", for instance – here **More Stars** – he might sometimes move away from the beautiful melody sung by Cornell Campbell, but never strays too far. The Heptones' "Soul Power" (**Sound and Power**), Jackie Mittoo's **West of the Sun**, Jerry Jones's interpretation of the Four Tops' **Still Waters** and Alton Ellis' "These Eyes" (**Those Eyes**) are among other Brentford Road standards to receive similar treatment – as do rootsier tracks like the Wailing Souls "Back Out" (**Black Man's Train**) and Burning Spear's "Pick Up the Pieces" (**Major Walk**). Besides Ranglin's mellow but inventive guitar – sometimes reminiscent of Wes Montgomery – Jackie Mittoo is much in evidence. A couple of tracks even feature melodica from Monty Alexander – the pianist who played the same local circuit of live and recording dates in the1950s before, like Ranglin, finding an appreciative international jazz audience.

➲ We almost chose **Roy Burrowes: Reggae Au Go...**, Studio One, US, 1995

68

Shabba Ranks

Golden Touch

Two Friends, 1990, JA; Greensleeves, 1990, UK

Recorded 1990. Shabba Ranks (deejay). Produced by Michael Bennett and Patrick Lindsay.

Like many of the rockstone-voiced deejays who emerged in the mid-1980s, Shabba Ranks – who was born Rexton Gordon in 1965, in St Ann's – first started to build his reputation with records for King Jammy. More unusually, he went on to surpass the quality of this early material with work for other producers. Jammy does deserve the credit for linking him with singers Home T and Cocoa Tea, but despite the brilliance of 1988's "Who She Love", the team was to have greater success with Gussie Clarke. Shabba shared his first album for Jammy with Chaka Demus, and if anything his colleague from Jammy's unassailable sound system seemed to be the stronger deejay.

Shabba's leap into the premier league came with a series of feisty singles for the man who had been the engineer on his material for Jammy. Encouraged by Shabba, Bobby Digital had set up his own Digital B label, and proceeded to catch the deejay at his most exciting on tough dancehall singles like "Peanie Peanie", "Hot Like Fire" and "Wicked In Bed" (collected on the *Just Reality* and *Best Baby Father* albums).

Bobby Digital was later to play a key role in the success of Shabba's albums for Epic. Before signing to the US major, however, the next port of call for Mr Gordon was Gussie Clarke's Music Works. There his international potential became more obvious, thanks to Gussie's glossy, more melodic rhythm, as well as the inspired pairing of Shabba's gruff tones with singers of the quality of J.C. Lodge, Krystal, Deborahe Glasgow, and, again, Cocoa Tea and Home T (see the very strong *Rappin' With the Ladies* and *Holding On* sets).

Another label for which Shabba recorded just prior to Epic was Michael Bennett and Patrick 'Shadow' Lindsay's Two Friends. This was an imprint – with a very similar sound to Gussie's productions – that never fulfilled its initial promise, but was at least responsible for Shabba's most consistent set, **Golden Touch**. To ensure variety, top studios in Kingston (Music Works and Black Scorpio), New York (FCF), and London (A-Class) were employed, and the world's most famous ragga dropped the easy option of 'slackness' (sexually explicit lyrics) to show just how inventive – and good humoured – he could be. Despite his reputation for slack material, Shabba had always interspersed pertinent commentaries on 'reality' themes – "Roots and Culture", "Just Reality", "Are You Sure" – amid the tunes that expressed more carnal concerns.

The most outstanding of the tracks on *Golden Touch* that have cultural topics – and one any traditional 'roots' follower should check – is **Build Bridges Instead**. The deejay adds his own heartfelt observations about the need for unity to Dennis Brown's finest record of the late 1980s, "No More Walls" (inspired by the collapse of the Berlin Wall). The final track, **Wicked In Bed – Part 2**, even takes a more sophisticated stance than that on the original "Wicked In Bed", suggesting that to be wicked in bed "yah mus' have somethin' inna yuh head."

Ragga's one international icon continued to make convincing records after signing to Epic, even if he inevitably lost ground with the hardcore dancehall crowd to such younger deejays as Buju Banton, Bounty Killer and Beenie Man. Wisely the US major continued to involve Bobby Digital in the production of Shabba's albums. To date, these have missed quite a few of the strongest singles to appear on the Digital B/Brick Wall labels – but perhaps they're being saved for a set of their own.

⮕ We almost chose **Rough & Ready Vol. 2**, Epic, US, 1993

69

Tony Rebel

If Jah

VP Records, 1998, US

Recorded 1997. Tony Rebel (deejay vocals) with rhythms from Firehouse Crew, Sly & Robbie, and others.

If Jah is a beautifully realized 1997 set from the deejay who, more than any other single figure, is responsible for the revival of cultural themes in today's dancehall. Although Tony Rebel (born Patrick Barrett, Manchester, Jamaica) had started out as a deejay in the early 1980s on sets like *Destiny Outernational* with Garnett Silk and Everton Blender, *Thunderstorm* and *Youth Promotion*, it wasn't until he began recording for Donovan Germain's Penthouse label that he started to make headway in the intensely competitive world of Jamaican music.

At Penthouse, Tony gained early hits like "Mandela Story" (1990) and a pairing with the label's then top deejay, Cutty Ranks, on the *Die Hard Pt. 1* album. He consolidated his position in 1991 with a string of hits; "Fresh Vegetable" on the Penthouse cut of "Love I Can Feel" was the most successful, but "The Herb", "War & Crime" and "Symptoms" all sold well, as did the combination DJ/vocal sides "Onward Christian Soldiers" (with his friend Garnett Silk) and "Respect & Honour" (with Beres Hammond). In 1992 Penthouse issued his first solo album, *Rebel With A Cause*. He also worked with Phillip 'Fatis' Burrell, Bobby Digital and Steely & Clevie, scoring for the latter with "Reggae Put Jamaica On Top" at the end of 1992.

US major CBS Sony had already signed deejays Cobra, Tiger,

and Super Cat, and in 1993 added Tony Rebel to the roster, issuing the *Vibes Of The Time* (1993) album. They tried to break all of the acts into the lucrative US hip-hop/urban market, and they went on to score a sizeable hit (750,000 sales) with Cobra's slack "Flex" single that year. But the cultural Rebel fared less well and, after being dropped by them in 1994, he established his own label, Flames. On it he has presented a range of new roots artists, including stalwarts like Everton Blender, along with relative unknowns like the promising Jah Mason.

If Jah offers a convincing demonstration of Rebel's mature deejaying style, in which he alternates melodic singjay couplets with hoarsely urgent chants. It comprises his own self-produced songs along with cuts recorded for 'Fatis' Burrell, Bobby 'Digital' Dixon, Donovan Germain, Richard 'Bello' Bell and Courtney Cole. **If Jah** – a song also known as "Jah By My Side" – is typical, voiced over a brisk modern rhythm played by Firehouse Crew. Other tracks use Bob Marley rhythms, reflecting an increasing trend in 1990s roots music; **Love Fountain** uses the "So Much Trouble" rhythm, while **Warning** is exactly that – with lines like "Marley and Silk dem did a warn/Garvey and the X did a tell you wha go gwan" – and rides Bobby Digital/Barry O'Hare's cut of Marley's "Heathen" rhythm.

More traditional dancehall rhythms are also represented; "The Lecture" underpins **Jah Will Never Let Us Down** while the visionary **Know Jah** is propelled by a furious digital cut of "Swing Easy", **Ready To Go**, a superbly integrated combination with Marcia Griffiths, blends the rhythms to the Heptones "Land Of Love" and Slim Smith's "Rougher Yet". The other combination is with dub poet Muatabaruka, a celebration of Africa designed to overcome negative images of war and famine. The whole set strikingly affirms Rebel's Rasta faith and 'conscious' approach, and also illustrates his desire only to record socially uplifting material. It's a credit to Rebel's skill and obvious sincerity that this didactic material never seems forced. A crucial statement from the heart of modern roots music.

⮞ We almost chose **Vibes Of The Time**, Chaos, US, 1993

70

Duke Reid/Various Artists

Duke Reid's Treasure Chest

Heartbeat, 1992, US/UK

Recorded 1966–70. Produced by Duke Reid. Artists include the Royals, Melodians, Jamaicans, Paragons, Silvertones, Ethiopians, Techniques, Sensations, Three Tops, Justin Hinds and the Dominoes, Phyllis Dillon, Alton Ellis, U-Roy, Dobby Dobson, Honey Boy Martin, Hopeton Lewis, Winston Wright, Girl Satchmo, Joya Landis.

By all accounts, Arthur 'Duke' Reid (1915–75) was a flamboyant and often intimidating character. A former policeman – a champion marksman at that – he got into the sound system business in 1954 through selling liquor. When Coxsone Dodd started his own sound the next year, the stage was set for a great rivalry. In the dancehall, Duke Reid was crowned 'King of Sounds and Blues' between 1956 and 1958. Coxsone then dominated until 1966, when rock steady emerged with Duke Reid as its foremost producer.

Duke Reid's Treasure Chest is exactly that – 33 of its forty tracks count as classic hits from mid-1966 to early 1968, the golden age of rock steady. Every one shows what a perfectionist Reid was – he would reject masters if they didn't sound right, and even use gunplay to get the required performance from his musicians. Although Hopeton Lewis' "Take It Easy" – recorded for Federal in 1966 – is usually cited as the first rock steady song, Duke soon became the genre's definitive producer. His productions were irresistibly dynamic and subtly shaded, his artists polished and soulful. His studio – in downtown Kingston on Bond Street above the Treasure Isle liquor store – was operational from late 1965 on, and its wood construction gave it a warm acoustic that proved tailor-made for rock steady. Duke's choice of musicians was similarly judicious. His studio band – often led by the late Tommy McCook and called the Supersonics – included hornsmen like Herman Marquis, Johnny Moore, and Danny Simpson. The rhythm – much slower than upbeat ska – was played on organ and piano, over crisply syncopated drum patterns augmented by guitarists like Hux Brown, Ernest Ranglin or Nearlyn 'Lynn' Taitt. Taitt's role was crucial; playing along with the bass line on the bass string of his guitar, he'd inject string effects – a percussive click or a springy glide – that became like a signature on the rhythm.

Alton Ellis's **Girl I've Got A Date** is a crucial transitional record. Certain ska elements are still present, like the brisk tempo and Charlie Organaire's harmonica on the afterbeat. What's new is the bass line, a syncopated repeated pattern rather than the insistent walking bass of ska. It slowed the tempo down and increased the emphasis on the interplay of the rhythm. Ellis was Treasure Isle's main solo star at this time, his soul-inflected timings proving more suitable for the new rhythm than the rural style of Justin Hinds and the Dominoes. Reid also had hits with Dobby Dobson – his poor boy classic **Loving Pauper** is included here – Ken Parker, and Vic Taylor, while Phyllis Dillon and Joya Landis easily equal the heights reached by Alton Ellis. Dillon's version of the 1940s standard **Perfidia** is sublime pop music and her sensual **Don't Stay Away** equally persuasive.

When rock steady is mentioned, however, most fans think of vocal groups; they're here in abundance. Two brilliant sides from the Paragons – the original of Blondie's **Tide Is High**, and a superb cut of **My Best Girl**, accompany songs of similar quality from the Melodians, Sensations, Three Tops, Silvertones and others. The set is rounded off by a handful of classy instrumentals, and a pair of definitive U-Roy toasts from 1970. All the cuts have been mastered from first generation tapes; the sound quality is as good as it gets, as is the music: as essential to a Jamaican music collection as Bob Marley or the Skatalites.

⮑ We almost chose **More Hottest Hits**, Heartbeat, US/UK

71

Winston Riley/Various Artists

Roots Techniques

Pressure Sounds, UK, 1999

Recorded 1969–76. Featuring Horace Andy, Johnny Osbourne, Jimmy Riley and others (vocals), Big Youth, I-Roy (deejays); Ansel Collins (keyboards), Soul Syndicate and the Mercenaries (aka Revolutionaries). Produced by Winston Riley.

Although barely recognized outside the Jamaican music community, a strong case could be made for arguing that Winston Riley has been the most successful producer in Jamaican music history. He alone has scored hits, both internationally and in the dancehall, in every decade onward from the 1960s. His career as a founder member of the Techniques vocal group is assessed elsewhere in this book (see p.165); **Roots Techniques** concentrates on his output as producer in the 1970s with some excellent vocals and versions, plus a brace of brilliant deejay tracks. As the CD title makes clear, the songs portray the reality of ghetto living and propose the system of Rasta belief – 'Rasta livity' – as means of surviving those harsh conditions.

Riley had an early breakthrough to international success in 1971, when Dave and Ansel Collins' deejay/instrumental hit "Double Barrel" reached number 1 in the UK. Dave (Barker), who earlier had cut fine sides for Lee Perry and Bunny Lee, proved himself an even more soulful singer on "Your Love Is A Game", where his beautiful, anguished vocal slithers convincingly over the insistent rhythm; in keeping with the overal theme of this intelligently compiled CD, this is a love song that actually questions the sincerity of 'love'. It's followed nicely by former Sensation Johnny Osbourne (he wrote UB40's hit

"Come Back Darling"), who delivers his superb **Purify Your Heart**, a deeply felt invitation to commit to Rasta beliefs. Osbourne, yet another underrated singer, also cut the similar "Warrior" for Riley around this time. Former Unique Jimmy Riley's **Prophecy** is another roots classic; the King Tubby-mixed dub is also included (three other songs here come complete with dubs mixed by him).

In 1973 Riley cut an instrumental with the Soul Syndicate; it was originally built for a Max Romeo vocal. The instrumental was named after a British war film about a POW camp called "Stalag 17"; the rhythm, powered by a brutal, nagging bass line from George 'Fully' Fullwood, has subsequently gone on to become one of the most popular in reggae history, with over 400 versions recorded so far. Two of the very best are included here; Big Youth's stirring **All Nations Bow**, in which he freely incorporates lyrics from the Last Poets, and Horace Andy's excellent **Love Is The Light**.

Of the remaining tracks, I-Roy's toast over the unknown vocal group on **Who Is The Man** is top-notch deejaying from a master of the craft. **Zion I**, sung by Winston himself with organ backing from Ansel Collins, recalls the deeply spiritual music of Yabby You; on the same rhythm, the haunting vocal **Nothing Is Impossible** by the Interns (aka the Viceroys) is heard immediately after, followed by a further melodica cut from Ansel Collins. The set closes with Morvin Brooks' subtly uplifting **Cheer Up Black Man** and its corresponding dub version, again mixed by King Tubby.

Several of the rhythms here – "Stalag", "Purify Your Heart", "Who Is The Man" – also crop up in dub versions on our second choice below, as the *Roots Techniques* booklet notes indicate. In fact Winston Riley has a wealth of such material awaiting reissue. Until then, this compilation fills a long-overdue gap. Hopefully Pressure Sounds will also treat us to similar compilations covering Riley's excellent 1980s dancehall output.

⊃ We almost chose **Techniques In Dub**, Pressure Sounds, UK, 1997

72

Max Romeo

Open the Iron Gate 1973–77

Blood & Fire, 1999, UK

Recorded 1973–77. Max Romeo (vocals) with Family Man Barrett (bass), Carlton Barrett (drums), Mikey Chung (gtr), Clive Hunt (kbds), and others. Engineered by Lee Perry and others.

Having cut his first records with the Emotions for Ken Lack's Caltone label in the late 1960s, Max Romeo notched up a UK top ten hit as a solo artist in 1969, with the rude "Wet Dream". That uncharacteristic waxing did little for his future standing with people outside the reggae world. Despite a couple of attempts to repeat its success with similarly risqué titles, his gospel-inspired vocal style was usually employed on far more serious 'cultural' expressions. The Derrick Morgan-produced "Let the Power Fall For I", which became a PNP electioneering slogan in 1972, was one example, as were more explicit Rastafarian outings such as "Public Enemy No 1" and "Babylon's Burning" for Lee Perry, and "Rasta Bandwagon", "Coming Of Jah" and "Fire Go Deh Bun" for Winston 'Niney' Holness. Further notable titles in a similar vein appeared for Prince Buster, Randy's, Pete Weston, Willie Francis, Rupie Edwards, 'GG' Ranglin, and Sonia Pottinger.

By late 1974, Romeo was recording at Lee Perry's Black Ark studio, then in full operation. The resulting tale of a party interrupted by a police raid, **Three Blind Mice**, was a major Jamaican hit the next year. It was followed in 1976 by "Sipple Out Deh" (aka "War In A Babylon") and "One Step Forward", both of which were well received by UK rock critics, at least once they appeared on a well-packaged Island album. In the same period as he cut "Three Blind Mice", Maxie was having equally memorable singles appear on a label called Black World. All of these were recorded at either the Black Ark or Randy's Studio 17, and at least a couple involved Clive Hunt (aka Azul) as arranger. Before 1975 was over, most of Romeo's Black World material was collected for the classic *Revelation Time* album, including the dubs of **Blood of the Prophet** and **Open the Iron Gate**, with "Three Blind Mice" completing the package. Curiously, however, he didn't see fit to include **Valley Of Jehosophat**, the heaviest of the Black World singles, and one destined to become a collector's item a decade or so later.

Now that the entire *Revelation Time* album has resurfaced as the core of the **Open The Iron Gate** collection on Blood & Fire, the legendary 'missing' track takes its rightful place, complete with its magnificent version side. The original dubs that appeared on the flips of the **Revelation Time** and **Warning Warning** singles are also added, emphasizing the strength of the original rhythms that Maxie used. Recorded between his trailblazing 'rebel music' singles of the start of the decade, and the *War In A Babylon* album of 1976, there was always an argument for seeing *Revelation Time* as his strongest set, featuring as it did some of his most incisive 'reality' lyrics and the kind of pared-down production best suited to his poignant vocals.

As though to prove the consistency of Maxie's 1970s work, the package includes another three extra tracks. The slightly earlier **Every Man Ought To Know** opens the set, while an alternate vocal to the "Sipple Out Deh" rhythm, **Fire Fi the Vatican**, and the breathtaking 1977 self-production **Melt Away** (in its original 12-inch mix), are tacked on to the end. Max Romeo has long been an under-acknowledged talent, and this CD makes the ideal introduction to his still relevant vision of life as experienced by the Jamaican majority.

⮑ We almost chose **War In A Babylon**, Island, 1976

73

Little Roy

Tafari Earth Uprising

Pressure Sounds, 1998, UK

Recorded 1972–78 at Randy's, Black Ark, Channel One & Harry J studios. Musicians include Aston "Family Man" Barrett (bass), Earl 'Chinna' Smith (gtr), Leroy Sibbles (piano), Pablo Black percussion), Carlton Barrett and Leroy Wallace (drums).

Little Roy (born Earl Lowe in Whitfield Town, Kingston, 1953) was one of the first vocalists to sing what would become known as roots music. He began his career with Prince Buster before trying his luck with Lloyd 'Matador' Daley while still at school. He and his friend Carly had a song they had written called "Bongo Nyah", which they recorded with Family Man and Carlton Barrett's band The Hippy Boys. It was a hit all over the Caribbean.

Little Roy went on to cut a dozen songs for Daley, including a hit reggae version of Bread's "I Want To Make It With You", but he really wanted to sing more Rasta-oriented cultural material. In 1972, like many other roots artists of the period, he started his own label, naming it Tafari, and over the next few years he released a series of singles, eventually collected on his first album *Tribal War* and released through his friends Munchie Jackson and Lloyd 'Bullwackie' Barnes in New York. That set has been used as the basis for **Tafari Earth Uprising**, a long-overdue reissue comprising twelve songs and two dubs.

The album features at least two bonafide classics. **Tribal War** is a deeply moving plea for peace, written as a response to the internecine gang war raging between political factions in Kingston's ghettoes in mid-decade. As a member of the Rasta organization the Twelve Tribes of Israel, Little Roy warned of the dangers in aligning with one side or another during a time of serious unrest. It was recorded at Lee Perry's Black Ark studio in 1974. When John Holt re-recorded the song for Channel One the next year it became a huge hit, spawning cover versions by George Nooks, Ronnie Davis, and Freddie McKay. 1974 also saw the release of Roy's other much-versioned song, Prophesy. This song was voiced on a 'Blacka' Morwell-produced rhythm, squeezed out of a Pete Weston session at Dynamic and featuring Joe White on melodica; a devastatingly simple rhythm, it is just discernible under Roy's heartfelt vocal. "Prophesy" itelf became a hit again in 1989 for Freddie McGregor, a recut with Steely & Clevie that resulted in a flood of versions.

Roy's lyrics – steeped in Bible learning and natural imagery – are those of a devoted Rastaman. His songs look at themes such as Columbus's 'discovery' of America (Christopher Columbus), the African origins of humanity (Don't Cross The Nation) and ruling class morality (Richman Laugh). Others are uplifting affirmations of faith – Earth, Jah can Count On I, and Mt T (this latter with the Heptones backing his vocal). Two other tracks – Forces and Working – are trio performances with singers Ian and Rock, recorded at Channel One in 1978.

Perhaps because these songs originally appeared on obscure 45s with limited distribution, their impact was diffused. Roy secured a record deal in the UK – the largest market for reggae in the 1970s – too late for success, and he subsequently spent long periods in New York. In 1990, spurred perhaps by Freddie McGregor's hit with "Prophecy", he released Live On, a fine album recorded in Florida with Jamaican musicians. Better still was *Longtime*, a modern roots album made in 1996 with UK producer Adrian Sherwood and showing his songwriting and light, throaty tenor intact. Tafari Earth Uprising makes it clear that he was already a significant artist some 25 years ago.

➲ We almost chose **Longtime**, On-U Sounds, UK, 1996

74

The Royal Rasses

Humanity

Ballistic, 1979, UK; God Sent, 1999, UK

Recorded 1975–78. The Royal Rasses: 'Prince' Lincoln Thompson (vocals), Cedric Myton (vocals), Keith 'Cap' Peterkin (vocals), 'Johnny Cool' Hall (vocals), Jennifer Lara (vocals). Produced by Lincoln Thompson.

In essence the Royal Rasses were always their songwriter and lead singer, the late 'Prince' Lincoln Thompson. As with Roy Cousins's Royals or Carlton Manning's Shoes, whoever sang the always immaculate harmonies, Thompson moulded their sound. He started out in the music business, however, as a member – with Devon Russell, Cedric Myton, and Lidberg 'Peps' Lewis – of the Tartans, who scored with the rock steady hit "Dance All Night". During the 1970s, Studio One released three classic singles, all credited to Prince Lincoln. "True Experience", "Live Up To Your Name" and "Daughters Of Zion" were reflective, under-stated roots tunes that sounded as though Thompson had recorded them primarily out of commitment to his Rastafarian faith.

Thompson gained a somewhat higher profile, and even flirted with crossover success, when he formed the Royal Rasses, initially with Cedric Myton, Keith 'Cap' Peterkin, and Clinton 'Johnny Cool' Hall. Other harmony singers involved in the group's fluid membership included the talented Studio One regular Jennifer Lara. The first couple of singles on God Sent, Kingston 11 and Love the Way It Should Be, were immediately acclaimed as classics by reggae aficionados. Their success led to a contract with Ballistic Records in the UK, who tried to sell the Royal Rasses' magnificent debut album, **Humanity**, to the crossover audience that then existed for roots reggae.

Perhaps Prince Lincoln tried just too hard for the elusive international audience; a couple of subsequent sets, including one with rock singer Joe Jackson, sold disappointingly in both the reggae and pop markets. Little more was heard from Lincoln Thompson until he set about rebuilding his career in the 1990s. The critical triumph of his *21st Century* album of 1998, which showed that he had lost none of his powers, made even more tragic his death from cancer the next year. His reputation will, however, always rest on *Humanity*, a consummate expression of his social, spiritual and musical vision. The reason it did not achieve a greater impact at the time must have lain in the number of tracks already released as singles. Only two of the seven were completely new, while several were presented in 'disco-mix' style, with vocals plus dubs; the inclusion of a couple more fresh tunes might have made all the difference.

Before the opening track, San Salvador, finally surfaced on vinyl, it was one of the most popular dubplates on Lloydie Coxsone's London-based sound system. Two decades later, it still sounds as momentous as when first heard. Its theme – the coming of Jah's destruction – might have been conventional enough, but the references to San Salvador certainly weren't, and pointed to Thompson's constant desire to push against the parameters of reggae. This is even more obvious in the melodies and imaginatively arranged harmonies found throughout. Soaring and swooping above everything to spine-tingling effect, Prince Lincoln's own high tenor is without compare in the entire field of reggae. For anyone possessing all the singles – the others were Unconventional People, Old Time Friends, "Kingston 11", and "Love the Way It Should Be" – one of the two previously unreleased tracks, They Know Not Jah, stands as easily their equal. An inspired set, *Humanity* can be placed alongside classic debut albums of roots harmonizing by the Royals, the Abyssinians, the Congos and the Mighty Diamonds.

➲ We almost chose **21st Century**, 1-5 South Records, UK, 1997

75

The Royals

Pick Up The Pieces

Wambesi, 1977, UK

Recorded 1973–77. The Royals: Roy Cousins (vocals), Errol Wilson (vocals), Keith Smith (vocals), Berthram Johnson (vocals) and others. Produced by Roy Cousins.

During the 1970s, the vocal trios of Jamaica were singing a different tune. Whereas the great rock steady groups, like the Paragons, Melodians, Techniques, and Heptones, usually performed soul-influenced love songs, those who came to prominence later sang predominantly cultural lyrics. Their music is characterized by well-crafted close harmony vocals and dignified Afrocentric themes. In the pantheon of roots trios, the Royals, founded in 1964 by Roy Cousins, belong in the first rank. They may be less well known than the Abyssinians, the Wailing Souls or the Meditations, but the Royals' output, although slimmer, easily matches them artistically.

"Save Mama", the debut by the Royals' original lineup – Cousins, Berthram Johnson, Keith Smith and Errol Wilson (aka Errol Nelson) – was issued in the UK on Blue Beat in 1964. They also made records for Duke Reid, Joe Gibbs, and others, cutting their first version of Pick Up The Pieces for Coxsone in 1967, who released it under the name of the Tempests.

Cousins started up his own Tamoki and Wambesi labels in 1972, while he was also working for the Jamaican Postal Service. Pick Up The Pieces collects a dozen of the Royals' best performances from this era. To build the rhythms, Roy used top-quality session musicians, including members of the Wailers band, Soul Syndicate, In Crowd and Now Generation. The group's personnel changed frequently; only Cousins remained constant. Errol Nelson left to form the Jayes, and later sang in Black Uhuru. King Tubby's brother Lloyd 'Scunna' Ruddock, Rudolph Reid, and Lloyd Forrester all passed through.

The sound of the Royals is really Roy's creation, setting his tenor or falsetto vocals against the harmonies of the backing singers. The songs – celebrations of Jah, homilies for righteous living, meditations about life from a ghetto viewpoint – are completely sincere, as demonstrated on the title song, **Pick Up The Pieces**. A recut of their original Coxsone recording, it opens with a full half-minute of wordless group harmony, in the manner of the US group the Impressions. Cousins then sings: "Pick up the pieces, don't throw it away / Pick up the pieces, let's put them together / Life can be beautiful / If you only only try to make it what it should be / You better not wait, better not wait / On time . . .". The cumulative effect is subtle but powerful, Cousin's deeply felt lead, with occasional lisp, and the impeccable harmonies transforming the somewhat commonplace lyric into a soulful, affecting plea. The lyric qualities of Cousins' songs shine through again and again on this satisfyingly coherent set including the impassioned **Sufferer Of the Ghetto**, the gentle argument of **Only For A Time**, and the subtly militant **Blacker Black**, even when the sentiments have been heard countless times before.

Roy secured a major-label deal in the UK, and United Artists subsidiary Ballistic licensed three albums – *Pick Up The Pieces*, *Ten Years After*, and *Israel Be Wise* - between 1977 and 1979. Both the Royals, and the similarly named Royal Rasses, who were also on Ballistic, eventually failed to reach the audience that had emerged with the international success of Bob Marley. As the '70s ended, the demand for roots trios slowly ebbed and Roy devoted more time to producing others, including Earl Sixteen, Prince Far I and the Meditations. He relocated to Liverpool, England, in the early 1980s, but has continued to reissue his large (and underrated) catalogue.

➲ We almost chose **Ten Years After**, Tamoki Wambesi, UK, 1996

76

Scientist/Linval Thompson

Scientist Meets The Space Invaders

Greensleeves, 1981, UK

Recorded 1981. Musicians include Gladstone Anderson (pno), Noel Bailey (gtr), Carlton Davis (drums), Errol Holt (bass), Wycliffe 'Steely' Johnson (organ), Eric Lamont (gtr), Valentine Scott (drums), Noel 'Skully' Simms (pcn), Sky Juice (pcn), Winston Wright (organ). Engineered by Scientist. Produced by Linval Thompson.

The mixing engineer known as Scientist was responsible for the most innovatory strides in the development of dub since the initial experiments of his mentor, King Tubby. Born Hopeton Brown in Kingston in 1960, Scientist started his apprenticeship with Tubby performing such humble tasks as winding transformer coils. His big break came when the main engineer at the Dub Master's Dromilly Avenue studio, Prince Jammy, was unable to finish a session with producer Errol 'Don' Mais. Though he's not sure which was the first hit he got to mix, Scientist remembers the teenage Barrington Levy's "Collie Weed", in 1979, as among his earliest efforts. The young engineer became known to the wider world when he was credited with mixing the same singer's ground-breaking *Bounty Hunter* set – the album that's usually recognized as kickstarting the 'dancehall' phase of the music.

Perhaps because dub had declined in popularity since the mid-1970s, few of the version sides of the singles that feature Scientist's distinctive style were credited to him. However, he soon became known beyond the Kingston scene through the release of half a dozen dub albums by the UK label Greensleeves. Each sported an eye-catching cover linking Scientist's name with striking imagery drawn from computer games, sports, horror movies and the like. Four employed rhythms from 'Junjo' Lawes, but the most exciting of them all, **Scientist Meets The Space Invaders**, was the first of a pair from Linval Thompson. Formerly one of Bunny Lee's stable of singers, Thompson was by then a producer in his own right, employing the same musicians as Lawes, and closely rivalling him for dancehall supremacy.

Practically all Scientist's early dubs are worth hearing, but this set of ten of Thompson's hardest tunes stands out both for its sheer freshness – the young apprentice was obviously getting a tremendous kick from boldly going to parts of Tubby's mixing boards that even the master had yet to reach – and the choice of rhythms. Thompson's session band, the Roots Radics, was then engaged in redefining the Kingston studio sound just as the Revolutionaries had done half a decade before.

Scientist's approach to mixing could not have been better suited to the already pared-down style of the most in-demand studio band of the time, or the very similar production styles of both Lawes and Thompson. The slower Radics rhythms they used were perfect for Scientist's minimalist style, of applying reverb to alternate drum beats or keyboard chords, and then punctuating the mixes with them – to often stomach-churning effect. Jamaican music had never been sparser, and the young 'apprentice master', as he'd been called by Mikey Dread, appreciated that this very quality should be made even more rawer and more threatening at the mixing board. Wayne Wade's strongest record since leaving Yabby You, "Poor and Humble", a massive hit in the UK reggae chart, is particularly deadly in its reincarnation as **Cloning Process**. The final track, **Quaser**, deconstructs Johnny Osbourne's "Kiss Somebody" in even more awesome style.

By the time of his last Greensleeves album in 1983, Scientist had left Tubby for the sophisticated mixing board at Channel One, where he continued mixing until the middle of the decade. Dub aficionados, however, will always remember him best for his truly radical work at Tubby's between 1980 and 1982.

➲ We almost chose **Dub In The Roots Tradition**, Blood & Fire, UK, 1996

77

Garnett Silk

Killamanjaro Remembers Garnett Silk

Techiku, 1995, Japan

Recorded 1992–93. Garnett Silk (vocals). Features Richie Stephens, Capleton, Luciano and Dennis Brown. Produced by Ricky Trooper (Killamanjaro).

With the death of Garnett Silk, in a fire caused by a gas cylinder explosion at his mother's house in 1994, Jamaican music lost the singer who represented the best chance of crossover success for roots reggae in a generation. This assessment has been borne out by the subsequent appearance of solo singers such as Jah Mali, Ras Shiloh, Satellite, and Rolex, and the vocal group Morgan Heritage, all of whom display strong Silk influences.

Born Garnett Smith in Manchester, Jamaica, in 1966, Silk began his career as a sound system deejay in the early 1980s, under the name Bimbo (or Little Bimbo). He was close friends with the deejay Tony Rebel (Patrick Barrett); the pair recorded for Derrick Morgan, and often voiced specials together. The songwriter Anthony Rochester, also from Manchester, was another former schoolfriend. At the end of the decade, Garnett signed a two-year contract with producers Steely and Clevie, who renamed him 'Garnett Silk'. An album was recorded in 1989, but not released at that time, and he returned to the country, discouraged with the music business.

It was in 1992, when Rebel introduced Garnett to producer Courtney Cole – studio owner and boss of the Roof International label – that his career on record really took off. His hits "Nothing Can Divide Us", "Spanish Angel", and a cover of

Johnny Nash's "I Can See Clearly Now" were all heavily played on Ocho Rios-based radio station Irie-fm. He joined up with producer Bobby Digital for his first album *It's Growing*, and further hits like "The Rod" and "Splashing Dashing". By now, Garnett was being touted as the 'next Bob Marley', despite his complete lack of vocal resemblance to the superstar. Something in the intensity of his delivery, the thrilling vibrato of his wide-ranging tenor voice, and the profoundly cultural songs – often penned jointly with Rochester and/or Tony Rebel – prompted many to see him as the leading contender for crossover success. Throughout 1993, hits such as "Seeing Zion" for Jack Scorpio, and "Mama Africa" for Richard Bell's Star Trail imprint, continued to flow. These songs and many others of similar quality were first released on Jamaican 7-inch and US/UK 12-inch releases; they are scattered widely on a dozen or so CDs and vinyl albums, most of which are well worth hearing.

Killamanjaro Remembers Garnett Silk, however, is different from the 'official' studio recordings. It features Garnett in full flow on a series of dubplates – one-off exclusive recordings on acetate discs – made for the famous Kingston sound system Killamanjaro, operated by selector Ricky Trooper. They were originally recorded as ammunition in the ongoing 'sound war' that rages among Jamaican sound systems. They show the singer in an informal setting, in the dancehall – a milieu that he had made his own – and actually in the process of re-introducing cultural themes into it.

On the programme, he delivers custom versions of many of his big hits, and is heard in combination with vocalists Dennis Brown, Luciano, Lukie D, Scatta and Richie Stephens as well as deejays Buju Banton and Capleton. Garnett sings over specially recorded rhythms and original Studio One dubplates, boosting the sound and crew in time-honoured custom; it's a special treat to hear him sing over the 1968 Coxsone original cuts of "Hi Fashion" or "Real Rock", and a striking affirmation of reggae's true roots in the dancehall.

⮑ We almost chose **Lord Watch Over ...**, Greensleeves, UK, 1997

78

Sizzla

Black Woman and Child

Greensleeves, 1997, UK; VP/Brick Wall, 1997, US

Recorded 1997. Sizzla (deejay) with Sly & Robbie (drums/bass), Jayward Jazwad (kbds), Danny Browne (gtr/kbds), Barry O'Hare (kbds). Produced by Bobby Digital.

Like fellow cultural chanters Capleton and Anthony B, the youth known as Sizzla (Miguel Collins) specializes in militant Rasta pronouncements, often expressing the tenets of the turban-wearing Bobo Dread cult. These he delivers in particularly fiery tones – hence the name, conferred upon him by producer Homer Harris, owner of the Jamstyle label.

After proving himself on the Caveman Hi-fi sound system, Sizzla came to the attention of record buyers with a series of uncompromising singles on Phillip 'Fatis' Burrell's Xterminator imprint. These included combination discs with the singer Cocoa Tea, and two other deejay adherents of the Bobo Dread doctrine, Jesse Jendau and Louie Culture. His own debut album, *Burning Up* (1996), confirmed his potential, though it was a slew of sensational singles released in 1997 that generated real interest in his work. His next Fatis-produced set, *Praise Ye Jah*, sold out as soon as it appeared in London and New York, and was picked up by the leading UK distributor, Jet Star.

Almost before anyone had time to wonder whether Sizzla could repeat the feat, Robert 'Bobby Digital' Dixon produced his **Black Woman and Child** album. Every bit as powerful as the single cuts, it gained a slight edge from its greater variety of rhythms. Formerly the chief engineer for King Jammy's studio on St Lucia Road, Bobby Digital had already built a formidable reputation as a producer, most notably with the hits that established both ragga's first icon Shabba Ranks, and the singer most commonly credited with starting the return to 'conscious' concerns in Jamaican music, the late Garnett Silk. His rhythms took in the minimalist, drum-driven variety favoured by hardcore deejays, but also more traditional reworkings of reggae classics.

Both were employed as backdrops for Sizzla's righteous rants on *Black Woman and Child* – which featured leading session musicians from several generations, including Sly and Robbie, the UK's master rhythm builder Jazwad, the saxophonist Dean Frazer, the percussionist Bongo Herman, and the trombonist Ronald 'Nambo' Robinson – as well as the Main Street label's owner Danny Browne on guitar, and Roof International's Barry O'Hare on drums, bass and keyboards.

One outstanding example of Bobby Digital's refashioning of vintage music is heard on Sizzla's tirade against Babylon's brainwashing, **Give Them the Ride**. The rhythm was first heard on the rock steady instrumental "The Lecture", though this version owes more to the Studio One dub cut "Teasing". The owner of the legendary Brentford Road studio, Clement Dodd, receives part of the composing credit, as he does on another five tracks, including **One Away**, a "Satta Massagana" cut that's comparable with Morgan Heritage's superb call for unity on the same rhythm, "Live Up". Yet another tune with its roots in the legendary Brentford Road studio, **Make It Secure**, rides the Soul Vendors' "Drum Song", with Dean Frazer's fine saxophone substituting for Jackie Mittoo's keyboard. Elsewhere, Mr Collins shows himself just as at home on hardcore ragga beats – check **No Time To Gaze** or **Mi Lord**.

References to turbans and Prince Emmanuel might seem esoteric, but the sheer conviction Sizzla brings to his music gives it far more universal appeal – as could lines about people in the West who big up their chest, when they're still in slavery.

➲ We almost chose **Praise Ye Jah**, Xterminator / Jet Star, UK, 1998

79

The Skatalites

Foundation Ska

Heartbeat, 1996, US/UK

Recorded 1964–65. The Skatalites: Don Drummond (trombone), Johnny Moore (trumpet), Roland Alphonso (tenor sax), Tommy McCook (tenor sax, flute), Lester Sterling (alto sax), Jackie Mittoo (pno/organ), Jerry Haines (gtr), Lloyd Brevett (bass), Lloyd Knibb (drums). Produced by Coxsone Dodd.

The Skatalites are still seen as the premier Jamaican instrumental band – although their ascendancy lasted little over a year, from June 1964 until late summer 1965. But their star burned very brightly. Decades after, they continue to influence successive generations of musicians, both in Jamaica and abroad. In fact, a version of the band tours to this day with some of its founders still playing.

Foundation Ska, as the title implies, features the original lineup, with tracks drawn mainly from the period when they provided backing for such as the Wailers, Stranger Cole and Ken Boothe, and Jackie Opel, and the band was augmented on occasion by Ernest Ranglin or Lynn Taitt (guitar), Dennis Campbell (tenor sax), and Bobby Gaynair (tenor sax). The majority of these players had been pupils at the Alpha Boys' School, a Catholic charitable institution run by nuns, and almost all had worked their way through the ranks of dance and tourist circuit bands of the 1940s and '50s. They were basically jazz players, well schooled in swing and bop, as well as other Afro-American and Caribbean forms like r'n'b, rhumba, cha cha and merengue.

The Skatalites recorded principally for Coxsone Dodd, Duke Reid, and Justin Yap, and this compilation concentrates on the sessions for Coxsone, the producer who had been most instrumental in their formation – and name. When future prime minister Edward Seaga picked up on ska to represent Jamaican culture at the New York World's Fair in 1963, Dodd encouraged the band to 'name the band projecting the word ska'.

The selections – all top-notch ska – are drawn from traditional mento and folklore melodies, and also movies, hot soul tunes and even the Beatles. Movie or TV theme tunes account for seven of the titles here, including spirited versions of the theme from **Exodus** and the excellent **Black Sunday** (from the Brazilian film *Black Orpheus*). Other tracks were derived from the Afro-Cuban repertoire – the band was particularly fond of Perez Prado and Mongo Santamaria. They also cover Hoagy Carmichael's **Old Rocking Chair** with Bajan vocalist Jackie Opel.

The Skatalites' original compositions were inspired by then-current events – **Christine Keeler** and **Scandal Ska**, for example, or **Fidel Castro**, a homage to the Cuban sometime revolutionary – and by their mutual interest in Rasta beliefs. Many of the musicians were frequent visitors to various Rasta camps in and around Kingston – evinced in such titles as **King Solomon**, **Addis Ababa** and **Don D Lion** here – and in **Woman A Come**, an early Rasta-derived lyric sung by Drummond's girlfriend Marguerita Mahfood, a professional dancer who was tragically murdered by the trombonist in the early hours of January 1, 1965.

After the group split in 1965, following serious internal differences and capped by Drummond's incarceration, Alphonso went on to lead the Soul Vendors for Coxsone. Tommy McCook led the rival Supersonics for Duke Reid. Drummond died on May 6, 1969, in Kingston's Belle Vue Asylum. The remaining members all subsequently enjoyed long careers (McCook and Alphonso died within months of each other in 1998) in various studio bands, but their contributions as Skatalites in the 1960s remain their lasting legacy.

⮑ We almost chose **Ska Bonanza**, Heartbeat, US/UK, 1991

80

The Skatalites

Ska-Boo-Da-Ba

Doctor Bird, 1966, UK; West Side, 1998, UK

Recorded 1964–65. The Skatalites and others: Roland Alphonso (tenor sax); Lloyd Brevett (bass); Baba Brooks (tpt); Karl 'Cannonball' Bryan (baritone sax); Dennis 'Ska' Campbell (tenor sax); Don Drummond (tmbn); Jerome 'Jah Jerry' Hines (gtr); Lloyd Knibbs (drums); Tommy McCook (tenor sax); Jackie Mittoo (pno); Johnny 'Dizzy' Moore (tpt); Lester Sterling (alto sax); Lynn Taitt (gtr); Ron Wilson (tmbn).

In Jamaican popular music history, precedence is ususally given to the crucial and pioneering role played by the great sound system owners, who became the first producers. Royalty like Clement 'Sir Coxsone' Dodd, Arthur 'Duke' Reid, Vincent 'King' Edwards and Cecil 'Prince Buster' Campbell. However, you could make an almost equal case for the creative enterepreneurial role played by the Chinese-Jamaican community, who did so much to expose the music outside Jamaica. By the early 1960s, the foundation sound system owners had been joined by several Chinese-Jamaican producers, including such as Byron Lee, Vincent 'Randy' Chin, Leslie Kong, Charlie Moo and Justin Yap.

Justin 'Philip' Yap's family ran a grocery business in Barbican and the fledgling producer's first efforts involved sessions with fellow Barbican homeboy Ephraim 'Joe' Henry. Jamaican music was changing – the boogie-based r'n'b was mutating into ska – and in 1962 Justin ventured into the studio to cut trumpeter Baba Brooks on a version of the Artie Shaw swing staple "Jungle Drums", renamed "Distant Drums". Justin got on well with the musicians – he paid double the going rate for sessions – and "Distant Drums" sold well. In 1963 he produced another

Barbican resident Fitzroy 'Larry' Marshall (see p.99) on a cover of Paul Martin's minor US r'n'b hit "Snake In The Grass". His Top Deck label was beginning to gain a reputation – and this would be consolidated by the sessions he held in 1964/5.

The consensus of opinion among ska aficionados has gradually swung round to considering the cream of the Skatalites work to be the brilliant series of records resulting from Justin's three sessions. He was, remarkably, just twenty at the time. Two of these sessions were held at Coxsone Dodd's Brentford Road studio. The first was an eighteen-hour session in November 1964; the second took place a couple of months later; while a third also took place in early 1965, at the radio station JBC. The results included both instrumental and vocal tracks, featuring young singers like Jackie Opel and the Deacons, which were originally released as 45s on Yap's Top Deck and Tuneico labels.

Twelve of the hottest instrumentals were then collected on the 1966 album, **Ska-Boo-Da-Ba**, released by Graham Goodall's Doctor Bird Records in the UK. This has long been considered the definitive album of ska instrumentals, with the band's stellar trombonist Don Drummond well to the fore. Five of the composing credits were his – Confucius, China Town, The Reburial, Smiling and Marcus Junior – and all employed the kind of minor-key melodies that were to be the trombonist's greatest legacy for future generation of Jamaican musicians, and notably the melodica/keyboards player Augustus Pablo. Ska was nothing if not eclectic, and alongside original compositions, the tracks drew from a typically wide range of sources: a Japanese pop hit, US r'n'b instrumentals, Duke Ellington compositions (a version of "Caravan"), and a traditional mento number.

The CD, reissued as part of West Side's programme of the complete Top Deck/Tuneico material, restores a couple of tracks long absent from the vinyl album, and adds alternate takes of Ska-Ra-Van and Lawless Street. So, once more, this is a disc that belongs in every collection.

➲ We almost chose **Ska-Ra-Van**, Westside, UK, 1997

81

Steely and Clevie

Play Studio One Vintage

Heartbeat, 1992, US

Recorded 1991–92; Steely (bass), Clevie (drums), with Earl 'Chinna' Smith (gtr), Ernest Ranglin (gtr), Dean Frazer (sax), Danny Browne (kbds), Robbie Lyn (kbds), Nambo (trombone), David Madden (trumpet), and others.

Steely (Wycliffe Johnson) and Clevie (Cleveland Browne) were the dominant drum and bass duo of dancehall from the mid-1980s to the mid-'90s, chalking up hit after hit at King Jammy's Waterhouse studio. This choice, however, **Play Studio One Vintage**, is the duo's absolute career high: an album that pays tribute both to their own roots and to Clement Dodd's label with brilliant versions of classic songs from Studio One's late 1960s heyday.

Although both players had been around from the late 1970s – Steely in Generation Gap and Roots Radics, Clevie in the Browne Bunch (with his equally talented brothers Danny and Dalton) and Freddie McGregor's Studio One Band – they really came into their own as part of the team in residence at Waterhouse. There, from 1986, they powered a series of dancehall hits, among them Admiral Bailey's "Punaany", Supercat's "Boops", Chakademus's "Young Gal Business", Shabba's "Ting A Ling" and Buju's "Love Mi Browning". In 1992 they went one better, scoring a massive international crossover pop hit with Dawn Penn's "No No No". This was a faithful re-creation of her own 1968 hit – a bluesy number – propelled into the mainstream by its use on a European TV car advert, having already been huge in the clubs. That Steely and Clevie could score with a relatively straight recut of Coxsone's 1968 version was remarkable. The only concession to 1990s taste was in the crisp recording and entertaining use of samples, which, as well as the inevitable James Brown ("Get on up"), made liberal use of U-Roy's "Wake the Town" and Alcapone's "Play It Back Jack".

The core of *Play Studio One Vintage* is the performances, vibrantly successful, of such ostensibly 'old' songs. In Jamaican terms they are merely classics – and the living tradition of dancehall, constantly reinvented through versioning. Steely & Clevie excel themselves on virtually every track here and show their respect in their authentic re-creations. The Clarendonians' He Who Laughs Last has Ernest Wilson and Peter Austin sounding unerringly the same as the original, as does the Silvertones' Smile – a brilliant rhythm which would propel Garnett Silk's "Hello Mama Africa" later in 1992. Equally successfully renewed are the Flames' I Was Born To Be Loved, the Cables' Be A Man and Heptone Leroy Sibbles' Fatty Fatty. This latter rhythm also carries Dean Frazer and David Madden's homage to Cedric Brooks' Money Maker; trumpeter Madden had also played on the orginal instrumental.

And so it goes on – on an album whose only flaw is that it could be twice the length. Alton Ellis's Ain't That Loving You gets the instrumental treatment on Steely & Clevie's own sizzling Hitomi. If anything, Marcia Griffiths' take on Melody Life is better than her original hit, while veteran pianist Theophilius Beckford can hardly contain his happiness, breaking into ribald laughter on the instrumental break of his 1959 boogie monster Easy Snappin. The musicianship throughout is exemplary; these old chestnuts are burnished with style and affection to sound brand new.

The Dawn Penn hit contributed to Steely & Clevie's further plans to build their own base. By 1995 their Studio 2000 was in operation, recording dancehall stalwarts like Don Yute and new roots contenders like Bushman (see p.35). Hopefully they will find time to make more albums like this – a similar tribute to the music of Duke Reid would be a dream.

➲ We almost chose **Freddie McGregor: Now**, VP, US, 1991

82

King Stitt

Reggae Fire Beat

Jamaican Gold, 1996, Holland

Recorded 1969–70. King Stitt (deejay). Musicians include Aubrey Adams (organ), Winston Wright (organ), Gladstone Anderson (pno), Ernest Ranglin (gtr), Hux Brown (gtr), Val Bennett (sax), Headley Bennett (sax), Clifton Jackson (bass), Gladstone Bailey (drums), Hugh Malcolm (drums). Produced by Clancy Eccles.

Before U-Roy took the original Jamaican art of rapping over records from the dancehall to the recording studio in a serious way, a handful of early deejays sometimes found themselves making discs. While legendary foundation figures like Count Machuki, Cuttings, and Sir Lord Comic cut the occasional tune – often uncredited – none recorded so often, or with such success, as King Stitt.

Born Winston George Sparkes, in Kingston in 1940, Stitt's face was seriously disfigured from birth, but he actually used these features to his advantage, proudly promoting himself as the 'Ugly One' (taking a cue from the Sergio Leone western *The Good, the Bad and the Ugly*). Like most deejays with a neat line in jivetalk, Stitt initially earned his reputation at dances at venues like Carnival Lawn, and in particular on Coxsone Dodd's Downbeat sound system. When he joined the sound in 1957, Machuki was still Coxsone's number one deejay. Stitt began to attract followers of his own, and eventually took the older deejay's place on the number one set.

Although he was a big draw at dances, Coxsone was unsure how King Stitt's talk would transfer to disc, and was not the first producer to put him before a studio mike. Dodd only recorded

Stitt in the wake of the deejay's first ground-breaking hits for Clancy Eccles in 1969, all of which are now collected on the exhaustive **Reggae Fire Beat** compilation.

Eccles, one of Jamaica's earliest singing stars, had turned to producing a couple of years previously, and Stitt's first tune for him, **Fire Corner**, was a version of Eccles' own vocal, "Shu Be Doo". Over a typically fast reggae rhythm of the time, dominated by the Hammond organ of Winston Wright, Stitt throws down his challenge: "No matter what the people say, the sound leads the way / it's the order of the day, from your boss deejay I King Stitt / So mop it from the top, to the very last drop."

This set the format for the rest of the Ugly One's biggest hits, including **Vigorton Two**, **Herbsman Shuffle**, and **Lee Van Cleef** – a few original catch phrases delivered in a declamatory tone, over the kind of atmospheric, up-tempo rhythm that was then finding favour in the UK as well as Jamaica. Listening to the album today, the contrast between Stitt's gruff shouting and subsequent deejays' riding of the rhythm is striking. Stitt, like all the early dancehall toasters, based his style on the jivetalk of American radio deejays. In the dance, these early mikemen tended simply to introduce the records, and then throw in the odd interjection to raise the level of excitement among the dancers. Stitt's performances on record were an extension of this practice, with his jivetalk spread over more of the track.

Anyone curious about the history of Jamaican music should listen out on **Dance Beat 1**, on which the deejay and producer Eccles wax nostalgic over the early days of dancehall, recalling the venues, promoters, and characters on the mike. Following Count Machuki's death a few years ago, King Stitt himself is now himself the best-remembered figure, a surviving link with a time that has almost slipped from memory. No actual recordings of an early Jamaican dance exist but the *Dancehall '63* album (below), recorded in the '90s, features Stitt introducing and deejaying Coxsone tracks in his original, Machuki-inspired style.

◗ We almost chose **Dancehall '63**, Studio One, US, 1996

83

The Techniques

Run Come Celebrate

Heartbeat, 1993, US/UK

Recorded 1965–68. Vocalists include Slim Smith, Frederick Waite, Franklyn White, Pat Kelly, Bruce Ruffin, Lloyd Parks, Ernest Wilson, Marvin Brooks, Junior Menz, Jimmy Riley and Winston Riley. Produced by Duke Reid.

Some of the greatest soul voices in Jamaica have passed through the ranks of the Techniques. During the group's most active period, between 1964 and 1974, lead singers included Keith 'Slim' Smith, Pat Kelly, Bruce Ruffin, Lloyd Parks, Ernest Wilson, Marvin Brooks and Jimmy Riley. The Techniques' founder, Winston Riley, first got together with Slim Smith, Frederick Waite, and Franklyn White in the early 1960s at a school concert. They eventually came to the attention of future JLP Prime Minister Edward Seaga, who linked them up with bandleader Byron Lee. Together, they cut two songs for Federal subsidiary Kentone that were included on a US-released album produced in Chicago by Carl Davis and Curtis Mayfield for Epic Records in 1964. Only when they began recording for Duke Reid the next year, however, did they really get into their stride. **Run Come Celebrate** covers their work for that producer in some depth, featuring three ska songs and thirteen bonafide rock steady classics in top-quality sound, mastered directly from the original tapes.

The Techniques cut a hit at their first session, the storming **Little Did You Know**, on which Slim Smith alternately chokes back his emotions and soars passionately over the other voices and a band including trumpeter Baba Brooks and reedman

Herman Marquis. They followed this with other ska hits, including I'm In Love, and two tracks not included here, "When You Are Wrong" and "Telling Lies". Slim Smith then left the group; before dying in tragic circumstances, he recorded solo for Coxsone and Bunny Lee, and as leader of the Uniques for Lee and Winston Lowe.

Riley next brought in former Paragon Junior Menz and Bruce Ruffin, to cut hits like the Curtis Mayfield adaptation Queen Majesty, Love Is Not a Gamble, and My Girl. Lloyd Parks also recorded with the group at this time. Ruffin in turn left, to pursue a successful solo career with Leslie Kong.

With Pat Kelly drafted in to complete yet another new lineup, the Techniques continued their run of hits with I'm In The Mood For Love, the 1968 Festival Song entry Run Come Celebrate, and another Mayfield adaptation, "You Don't Care". Kelly's perfect falsetto can also be heard on It's You I Love and the beautifully realized cover of the Temptations' I Wish It Would Rain. Kelly promptly departed, returning to Bunny Lee for whom he cut a series of hits, beginning with "How Long" in 1969. He continued successfully with producer George 'Phil' Pratt and others until the mid-1970s, when the sweeter, soul-derived style he favours was temporarily superseded by the more militant 'roots and culture' music. Still an excellent singer, he continued performing and recording, and has participated in reunion shows by the group in recent years

The performances on *Run Come Celebrate*, together with similar ones from the same period by the Paragons, Alton Ellis, and the Melodians, epitomize rock steady at its best. The combination of soulful vocals, blending seamlessly with the rhythms – sweet but also heavy – of Tommy McCook's Supersonics, proved irresistible in the dancehalls of the day. They are the bedrock on which later developments such as dub and deejay were founded; thus U-Roy's first three deejay hits, which dominated the Jamaican charts in early 1970, used versions of smashes by Ellis, the Paragons and the Techniques for their backing tracks.

⮑ We almost chose **More Hottest Hits**, Heartbeat US/UK, 1994

84

The Tennors

Rock Steady Classics

Nighthawk, 1998, US

Recorded 1967-75. Vocalists include George 'Clive' Murphy, Maurice 'Professor' Johnson, Ronnie Davis, Norman Davis, Milton Wilson, Howard Spencer, Nehemiah Reid, George Dekker. Produced by Coxsone Dodd, Duke Reid, Sonia Pottinger, Bunny Lee and George 'Clive' Murphy.

The Tennors started off as a duo featuring George 'Clive' Murphy and Maurice 'Professor' Johnson; by early 1967 they had become a trio with the addition of Norman Davis. Their debut for producer Coxsone Dodd, **Pressure and Slide**, was one of the most popular tunes of 1967; it was also an early salvo in the 'version war' between rival producers, in this case Dodd and perennial rival Prince Buster. The ever-combative Prince had first cut the rhythm for his "Shaking Up Orange Street", itself intended as a reply to Dodd's Soul Vendors release "Whipping The Prince". Since then, there have been numerous recuts, including the Tennors' huge hit, included, of course, on **Rock Steady Classics**. Later hits on the rhythm include Sugar Minott's celebrated pro-herb anthem "Oh Mr. D.C." and deejay U-Brown's "Please Doctor", two of the biggest hits of 1979.

After Maurice Johnson was killed in an accident late in 1967, Clive decided to start his own label, called, not surprisingly, Tennors. Milton Wilson replaced Johnson, and the group began recording in WIRL Studios, cutting the double-sided hit **Ride Yu Donkey** and **Cleopatra** at their first session. Clive continued to release records on the Tennors label, but the group also recorded for other producers. Some of that varied output – for

Duke Reid (a beautiful cover of Simon and Garfunkel's **Weather Report**, and **Hopeful Village**) and Mrs Sonia Pottinger (**Give Me Bread** and **Gee Whiz**) – is included here, as are several tunes that originally appeared as solo records by Ronnie Davis, an excellent vocalist with a range similar to that of John Holt.

Davis had sung in rehearsal sessions with the Tennors before their breakthrough hits, but had returned dispirited to his country home in Savannah-La Mar, Westmoreland, rejoining when they began recording for Reid in 1968. Solo Davis titles here include **World Is A Stage**, **We Got Soul**, and **Good News** (a recut of John Holt's "Sad News", done for Bunny Lee in 1974). Ronnie also cut **Baby Come Home** in 1975 for Lloyd 'Spiderman' Campbell. After his days in the Tennors, he led the Itals roots trio from 1976, with Keith Porter and Lloyd Ricketts, who had been in an obscure vocal group called the Westmorelites in 1967 with Davis and Roy Smith. Porter and Ricketts recorded "Miss Hitie Titie" under that name for Studio One that year. The Itals had a string of hits in the mid-1970s with producer Campbell, making albums for the US independent label Nighthawk and achieving a Grammy nomination with their 1987 set *Rasta Philosophy*. A new group – Ronnie Davis and Idren, featuring Ricketts and Roy Smith, plus new member Robert Doctor, also from Westmoreland – started in 1996.

The Tennors might stand as emblematic for all the semi-forgotten vocal groups of rock steady and reggae. The trajectory of such groups – others include the Termites, the Hi-Lites, the West Indians and the Cables – follows a predictable pattern. After starting out with a few big hits, confined to the local scene, they prove unable to sustain that success, despite continuing to make excellent generic records. Ultimately, perhaps lacking an image, they split up. All that remains is a handful of superb and often rare 7-inch singles, perhaps an album or two, to mark their presence in the world's most productive music business. Sometimes, as in this case, that can be enough to deserve lasting recognition.

➲ We almost chose **Termites: Do The Rock Steady**, Heartbeat, US, 1991

85

Third World

Reggae Ambassadors

Island/Polygram Chronicle, 1993, UK/US

Recorded 1975–92. Third World: Michael 'Ibo' Cooper (kbds), Stephen 'Cat' Coore (gtr), Irvin 'Carrot' Jarrett (pcn), William 'Bunny Rugs' Clarke (vocals), Willie 'Root' Stewart (drums), Richie Daley (bass), Milton Hamilton (vocals), Cornel Marshall (drums). Producers include Chris Blackwell, Stevie Wonder, and Third World.

After Bob Marley's massive success with *Natty Dread* in 1975, the doors were open for similar self-contained groups to reach the global market. The Wailers' album was the first key statement of what dub poet Linton Kwesi Johnson called 'international reggae'. In an article in the UK theoretical journal *Race Today*, in 1976, Johnson characterized it as incorporating "elements from popular music internationally. Rock and soul, blues and funk, these elements facilitated a breakthrough on the international market." While taking nothing away from the likes of Steel Pulse, Inner Circle, Zap Pow, and Aswad, Third World were the first and best of all the 'international reggae' bands. For well over 25 years, they have been playing to appreciative audiences all over the world; indeed, though often dismissed as inauthentic by purists, the style has considerable claims to being the longest-lived in reggae history. The two-CD set **Reggae Ambassadors** covers their entire career, from their debut album right up to the 1990s.

The Third World story begins in the late 1960s, when two classically trained musicians, keyboard player Michael 'Ibo' Cooper and guitarist Stephen 'Cat' Coore, teamed up with the Lewis Brothers as part of Inner Circle. By 1973, Cooper and

Coore had left Inner Circle to form Third World, with a lineup augmented by percussionist Irvin 'Carrot' Jarrett, singer 'Prilly' Hamilton, bassist Richie Daley and drummer Cornel Marshall. Their first single, the soul-influenced Railroad Track, was released on their own Cavlip imprint.

Third World travelled to London, where Island boss Chris Blackwell saw them play live, and signed them up. Opening for Bob Marley on the historic 1975 European tour, they played at the legendary Lyceum concert. By the time they came to record their eponymous debut set, which featured an excellent cover of the Abyssinians' Satta Massagana, Marshall had been replaced by Willie 'Root' Stewart. Shortly afterwards, Bunny Clarke was added as new lead singer. Their second set, *96° In The Shade*, included a cover of Bunny Wailer's Dreamland, as well as the ambitious 96° In The Shade itself, whose lyric dealt with Jamaican hero Paul Bogle and his role in the 1865 Morant Bay rebellion against the British. Clarke had recorded for Lee Perry under the name Bunny Scott (aka Bunny Rugs); his lead vocals were a major factor in the success of their next album, whose title track, Journey To Addis, was a version of Don Drummond's ska classic "Addis Ababa". Clarke's vocal input was most apparent on their smooth version of the O'Jays Now That We've Found Love, in which Philly soul and reggae perfectly combined to create a massive worldwide chart hit.

After five albums for Island, Third World made five more for CBS during the 1980s. They signed next with US major Mercury for two albums; *Serious Business* (1989), and *Committed* (1992); the latter featured veteran Skatalites Roland Alphonso and Tommy McCook, as well as ragga deejay Terror Fabulous.

Previously unavailable minor masterpieces on the beautifully presented, musically diverse *Reggae Ambassadors* set include their debut single Railroad Track and some rare b-sides, but it was compiled too early to include 1997's superb Jamaican Taxi 45, "Dem Man Deh". Perhaps the title of the Niney-produced track from 1981 sums them up best of all – Roots With Quality.

⮞ We almost chose **96° In The Shade**, Island, UK, 1976

86

Peter Tosh

The Toughest

Heartbeat, 1996, US/UK

Recorded 1964–70. Peter Tosh (vocals) with Bob Marley (vocals), Neville Livingstone (vocals), U-Roy (deejay). Produced by Coxsone Dodd and Lee Perry.

Bob Marley and Neville 'Bunny Wailer' Livingston first met up with Peter Tosh in 1963. He played guitar and sang in a baritone voice that the other two thought would blend perfectly in the vocal group they wanted to form. Born Winston Hubert McIntosh, in Westmoreland in 1944, Tosh also taught Bob Marley how to play the guitar. Percussionist Alvin 'Seeco' Patterson introduced the group, who at this point numbered five members, to Clement 'Coxsone' Dodd. Like Tosh, the producer was a country man; he recognized and liked the rootsy, mento-influenced rural sound evident in Peter's vocal style. Between 1964 and 1967, the Wailers recorded prolifically for Dodd. **The Toughest** collects nearly all the songs on which Peter Tosh sang lead or joint lead – of issued titles, only a beautiful version of the folk song "Lemon Tree" is missing – together with five songs cut for Lee Perry during the period 1968 to 1970.

Like the Heartbeat Wailers' compilation *One Love At Studio One*, which covers a similar time period in the development of the main group, this set not only helps to clarify subsequent developments in the career of Peter Tosh, but also delivers powerful music in its own right. Several of the songs here were to figure prominently in Tosh's stage performances during the last ten years of his life.

Many of the early Studio One sides are ska adaptations of folk, mento and even Christian songs. There's also one cover, Peter's first attempt at Smokey Robinson's **Don't Look Back**, originally performed by the Temptations. Starting with the Toots-influenced **Hoot Nanny Hoot**, from 1964, we can hear Tosh learning his trade as vocalist. Later he tried his hand at calypso and folk material like **Shame and Scandal** and **Maga Dog**, the more spiritual **Amen** – again with a strong Toots style – and the soulful proto-rock steady **Sinner Man**. **Rasta Shook Them Up** was written just after Haile Selassie I visited Jamaica, and recorded in May 1966. Tosh warns that the wicked will "get their eternal pay", a theme he was to pursue with increasing militancy in his later years. Also present is Tosh's biggest hit of the 1960s, the boastful **I'm The Toughest**.

The fascinating Lee Perry material catches Peter just before the Wailers signed to Island Records in 1972. He also recorded for Joe Gibbs at this time, with results now also reissued by Heartbeat. **Brand New Secondhand** is a scathing attack on a girl, presented here in an extract from the session with a run-through and the issued version. The powerful **Down Presser** revisits "Sinner Man", while on the early deejay track with U-Roy – **Earth's Rightful Ruler** – Tosh interjects occasional comments and the Amharic introduction. **No Sympathy** was issued on an Upsetter-produced Wailers album, while the anti-colonial **400 Years** was covered by the full group on their major-label debut set for Island, *Catch A Fire*, in 1973.

After they left the Wailers, both Peter Tosh and Bunny Wailer made some great music, but neither managed to get his respective career on the same course as Bob. Peter signed with Virgin for two albums, then with the Rolling Stones label, issuing three moderately successful albums. He then signed with EMI and toured intermittently. His last album, *No Nuclear War*, won a Grammy award in 1988, but tragically, the success came too late. For reasons which have yet to be fully explained, Peter Tosh was murdered – shot by a former friend – on September 11, 1987.

➲ We almost chose **Peter Tosh: Honorary Citizen**, Sony Legacy, US, 1997

87

The Uniques

Watch This Sound

Pressure Sounds, 1998, UK

Recorded 1967–68. The Uniques: Keith 'Slim' Smith (vocals), Lloyd 'Charmers' Tyrell (vocals), Jimmy Riley (vocals). Produced by Bunny Lee and the Uniques.

Keith 'Slim' Smith (1948–73) was a definitive rock steady vocalist. Despite being heavily influenced by US soul singers like Sam Cooke, he had his own unmistakeable style from early in his career. Smith started out as one of the Techniques; on their 1965 song "Little Did You Know", his high tenor – insistent, emotion-wracked – grabs the attention immediately, soaring over the other voices. By late 1966, and the arrival of rock steady, he was ready. With Franklyn White, he left the Techniques to form the first version of the Uniques with Roy Shirley. That didn't last; Shirley was at the peak of his popularity as a solo artist, recording for Bunny Lee and others, while Slim too was making his own solo discs.

In late 1967, the Uniques re-formed, with a lineup of Slim, his former schoolmate Jimmy Riley, and Lloyd 'Charmers' Tyrell, who was later to become a very good and successful producer. This incarnation made the series of records during 1967 and 1968, mostly for producer Bunny Lee, which are anthologized on **Watch This Sound**. They rank among the most soulful vocal trio performances ever committed to wax in Jamaica. This was a transitional phase in Jamaican music when rock steady gave way to reggae, thanks to a new generation of hustling independent ghetto-based producers like Bunny Lee, Lee Perry, and Clancy Eccles.

Bunny Lee was a master at making something good from limited resources; unable to afford the most in-demand musicians, he utilized men like veteran saxist Val Bennett, guitarist Bobby Aitken, and a young group from his home turf of Greenwich Farm, the Hippy Boys. Thus began the careers of soon-to-be Upsetters Glen Adams and Aston 'Family Man' Barrett and his brother Carlton – the future Wailers rhythm section.

Of the two Curtis Mayfield songs here, both **Gypsy Woman** – quintessential rock steady – and **My Woman's Love**, with a beautiful falsetto vocal, easily bear comparison with Mayfield's versions, while originals like **Can't Do Without It** are near-perfect pastiches of his style. As for Stephen Stills' "For What It's Worth", Slim almost makes the song his own, as **Watch This Sound**. Sitting comfortably alongside the covers are several more songs penned by the Uniques, such as **Speak No Evil**, the oft-versioned **My Conversation**, and **Let Me Go Girl**, which reveal the writing abilities not only of Slim, but also of Riley and Charmers. Another standout is Slim's reworking of Bible verses in **The Beatitude**, with Val Bennett's sonorous honks adding a distinct ska dynamic to the already-buoyant rhythm.

Although well received in the reggae market, the tunes never crossed over to a wider audience. After the Uniques split, however, all three pursued successful careers as solo singers. Frustration was a part of Slim's life; in 1973, a project with Alton Ellis for UK major A&M never materialized, and the gig went to Ken Parker. Later that year, Slim cut a tune for Bunny Lee called "The Time Has Come", with Stranger Cole and Tony Mack on backing vocals. After the session he became mentally disturbed; according to producer Winston Riley, he had been given a spliff containing powdered lizard tail. That night, Slim turned up at his parents' house demanding entry; frightened, they refused. He attempted to break in, cut his arm in the process, and bled to death before help came. Tantalizing though it may be to speculate what might have been had he lived, the recordings he left testify to a singer of rare brilliance and supreme soul.

➲ We almost chose **Slim Smith: Out Of Love**, Cutting Edge, Japan, 1996

88

U-Roy

Version Of Wisdom

Virgin Frontline Classics, 1990, UK

Recorded 1970–71. U-Roy (deejay). Produced by Duke Reid.

U-Roy broke the mould of Jamaican music decisively and irrevocably in 1970, when three records included on **Version Of Wisdom** – Wake The Town, Rule The Nation and Wear You To The Ball – occupied the top three positions on the Jamaican chart for six weeks. Deejay music – essentially rapping over specially mixed rhythm tracks – had arrived. The story actually begins two decades earlier, with the MC Winston Count Machuki. Using a blend of Harlem jivetalk and slang picked up from US r'n'b radio disc jockeys, he introduced the records on the Sir Coxsone Down Beat sound system. Like his follower King Stitt, Machuki had his own catch phrases to hype up the tracks and get the crowd going. With the addition of vocal percussion effects – 'peps' – this was the early MC style. U-Roy was a big fan of Count Machuki; deejaying the sound called Doctor Dickie's Dynamic in the early and mid-1960s, before he started recording, he used such Machuki phrases as "Live the life you love, love the life you live, music alone is mine to give."

By 1968, U-Roy was playing rock steady hits on Sir George The Atomic. As his reputation increased, he was approached by Clement Dodd to deejay the number two set on Sir Coxsone Down Beat (King Stitt controlled the number one). He then returned to Sir George, before linking up with soundman Osbourne 'Tubby' Ruddock in 1969.

Tubby, a trained electronics engineer, used to repair faulty equipment in Duke Reid's studio, and was also invaluable in maintaining Reid's sound system. He was thus in a position to cut instrumental versions of Reid's rock steady classics for use on his own sound, the Home Town Hi-Fi, based in the Kingston ghetto of Waterhouse. The concept of making such 'dubplates' had come from a sound system owner in the old capital, Spanish Town – Rudolph Redwood, of Ruddy's Supreme.

The combination of these special dubplates and U-Roy enabled Tubby's sound to rule Jamaican dancehalls. By 1970, the set was billed as "King Tubby's Hi-Fi with U-Roy", and packing them in whenever he picked up the mike. No deejay had ever 'ridden' a rhythm like U-Roy; his rich-toned voice totally dominated proceedings, and invested the old rock steady hits with a completely new lease of life. After singer John Holt heard him in the dance, riding a version of one of Holt's hits with the Paragons, he told Reid, who requested a meeting. U-Roy had already recorded for Keith Hudson, Lloyd 'Matador' Daley and Bunny Lee. As a follower of Rastafari, however, he was not keen to work with Reid, because of the producer's formidable reputation for gunplay and his hostility to Rasta beliefs. Nonetheless, eventually he recorded two tunes at his first session, versions of Alton Ellis' "Girl I've Got A Date" ("Wake The Town") and the Techniques' "Love Is Not A Gamble" ("Rule The Nation"). Both gained considerable radio play and became monster hits.

A few weeks later, U-Roy recorded his version of the Paragons' "Wear You To The Ball", with its "chicka-bow, chicka-bow, chicka-bow-wow-wow" refrain. It followed the other two to the top of the charts. Numerous imitators began to appear, from Dennis Alcapone onwards, who recorded for Reid with similar success. Thus U-Roy's contribution was doubly significant. Not only did he introduce a completely new form – talking over rhythms – but he also laid down the classic deejay style, inspiring successive generations of deejays to take up the mike and rap, years before the US variant arrived on the scene.

⮑ We almost chose **The Lost Album ...**, Sound System, US, 1999

89

Bunny Wailer

Blackheart Man

Island, 1976, UK; Mango Reggae Refreshers, 1990, UK

Recorded 1976. Bunny Wailer (vocals), with Tommy McCook and Herman Marquis (sax), Peter Tosh (gtr), Carlton Barrett (drums), Aston Barrett (bass), Tyrone Downie (kbds), and others. Produced by Bunny Wailer.

Bunny Wailer (born Neville O'Riley Livingstone, Kingston, 1947) was a key and founding member of the Wailers. During their spell with Coxsone in the 1960s, he wrote and soulfully sang some of the most accomplished love songs they ever recorded, most notably the sublime "Sunday Morning". He also applied his Curtis Mayfield-tinged tenor to the rudeboy anthem "Let Him Go (Rude Boy Get Bail)", as well as a couple of socially conscious songs – the beautiful "I Stand Predominate", and "He Who Feels It Know It".

By the early '70s, Bunny's romanticism had been transformed into something more consistently spiritual, and after the Wailers signed to Island Records in 1972, he had enough money to launch his own Solomonic label in Jamaica. **Blackheart Man**, his 1976 debut album, gave the fullest expression to his strongly held Rastafarian beliefs – its title refers to how the Jamaican majority had traditionally seen the Rastaman, and how indeed had Bunny himself before his conversion in the late 1960s.

While many of the reggae albums financed by UK record companies in the mid-1970s were hopelessly compromised, *Blackheart Man* was one of the great successes, and arguably remains the strongest 'solo' album from any of the Wailers. Very obviously a set on which much time and thought had been expended, it was lavishly presented (at least by reggae standards). Both its original Jamaican and UK pressings came in gatefold sleeves, complete with printed lyrics, and it was clearly aimed far beyond the confines of the dancehall.

The contents more than lived up to the packaging. The ten reflective songs were the finest Bunny had written – from the sublime repatriation plea Dreamland, a fresh treatment of the song he had recorded with Scratch four years earlier, through the recent Jamaican hits Bide Up, Fighting Against Conviction (originally titled "Battering Down Sentence", and inspired by Bunny's own brush with the police over herb possession) and Rasta Man, to new songs of equal worth, including Blackheart Man itself, Armagedeon (Armagedon), and Reincarnated Souls. In contrast with the anger of Peter Tosh's output, this was material born of the same Jamaican ghetto suffering, but proclaiming some sort of spiritual resolution. Significantly, the album closes with Bunny's adaptation of This Train, a traditional Afro-American song that has always possessed both a temporal and religious meaning.

The treatments given this inspired material could not have been more considered. The list of musicians gathered for the sessions confirmed that this was meant to be something rather special. Alongside such stalwarts of the Kingston session scene as Tyrone Downie, Harold Butler and Winston Wright on keyboards, Tommy McCook, Bobby Ellis, Dirty Harry and Herman Marquis on horns, and Robbie Shakespeare playing bass on half of the tracks, there were several members of the group Bunny had helped to found – with Carlton Barrett on drums, and his brother, Aston 'Family Man' Barrett, responsible for another four of the bass lines. Bob Marley contributed to the backup vocals on one track, while Peter Tosh sang on several, as well as playing rhythm guitar, melodica and harmonica.

It was an immediate and enduring classic, born of a time when anything seemed possible for Jamaican music.

➲ We almost chose **Sings The Wailers**, Mango, US, 1980

90

Wailing Souls

Wild Suspense

Island, 1995, UK

Recorded 1976–77. Musicians include Sly Dunbar & The Revolutionaries. Produced by Jo Jo Hookim.

Though they have undergone various changes throughout their thirty-year career, the core of the Wailing Souls has always been Winston 'Pipe' Matthews and Lloyd 'Bread' Mcdonald. Still active, they were probably the island's most consistent harmony group through the 1970s and '80s, and they have an influential role in reggae history, having started out in Trenchtown (as The Renegades) alongside the Wailers.

The duo debuted in the late 1960s as backing vocalists for a couple of Ernest Ranglin albums. Then from 1969, with George Haye, and later Oswald Downer and George Davis, they made a series of recordings at Studio One (which still await reissue on CD) and cut some songs (notably "Gold Digger") for Lloyd the Matador. In the early 1970s they made "Harbour Shark" as Pipe and the Pipers; sang backup harmonies on the Wailers' immortal "Trenchtown Rock"; and then had a spell with Joe Higgs as part of the group Atarra. The group reverted to the Wailing Souls identity when Higgs left to tour with Jimmy Cliff, and joined forces with what was rapidly becoming the leading studio in Jamaica, Channel One. **Wild Suspense** represents some of the fruits of their sojourn at the studio, recorded during 1976–77 at the Maxfield Avenue premises, which at the time was virtually a war zone in the heart of the ghetto.

They began at Channel One by recutting some of their Studio One classics like **Things & Time** and **Back Out**, as well as new songs **Joy Within Your Heart** and the 12-inch version of **Very Well**. Rudolph 'Garth' Dennis joined the lineup at this time, replacing Downer and Davis, and the group started their own label, Massive, releasing tracks like **Bredda Gravalicious** and **Feel The Spirit** that were both artistically succesful and strong sellers, with the trademark harmonies of the four-man group contributing in no small measure to this success.

Island Records first released the *Wild Suspense* album in 1979 and it was universally and warmly praised. Aside from the songs already noted, Garth Dennis revisited his 1972 recording **Slow Coach**, and from the Studio One days they also recut **Row Fisherman** and **Walk But Don't Fall**, as well as new material. This CD also includes seven previously unreleased dubs, including a stunning seven and a half minute version of "Very Well".

By 1980 the Wailing Souls had shifted allegiance to Sly Dunbar's Taxi label, cutting the hits "Sugar Plum Plum" and "Old Broom" for him. As the focus of Jamaican popular music shifted back to the dancehall, they began working with leading producers in that style like Henry 'Junjo' Lawes and Linval Thompson, and their offerings were always a cut above most of the opposition; indeed, John Holt recorded Pipe's composition "Sweetie Come Brush Me" and revived his own career into the bargain. Superb albums for Junjo – *Fire House Rock* (1980) – and Linval Thompson – *Wailing* (1981) – followed.

After Bob Marley's death in 1981, the mainstream media lost interest in reggae. Undeterred, the Wailing Souls continued recording through the decade, issuing a brace of fine albums for the Washington-based producer Delroy Wright (*Lay It On The Line*, 1986 and *Kingston 14*, 1987), and *Stormy Night*, an excellent 1989 set for King Jammy. In the early 1990s, Matthews and McDonald signed with Sony subsidiary Chaos and had another try at crossover with *All Over The World*; it may have lost them some of their old roots fans, but it showed their abilities as a harmony group undiminished.

➲ We almost chose **Fire House Rock**, 1980, Greensleeves, UK, 1992

91

Delroy Wilson

Original Twelve

Heartbeat, 1991, US/UK

Recorded 1966–68. Delroy Wilson (vocals). Produced by Coxsone Dodd.

Delroy Wilson (1948–96) was one of the half-dozen classic soul voices of Jamaican music. He was already a child star when he started recording for Studio One in 1963, in the early days of ska. Of the sound system war between label owner Coxsone Dodd and rival Prince Buster, Delroy once said "It look like I was the missile." The tunes he made at the time – "Spit In The Sky", "Joe Liges", "King Pharaoh" – all aimed straight to the head of Buster.

Many were collected on *I Shall Not Remove*, Wilson's first album for the label. When his voice broke, he continued making hits for Studio One until the late 1960s. The best of these are available on two albums, *Good All Over* and the **Original Twelve** set, the latter of which is reissued on this Heartbeat CD with two of its tracks in extended 'discomix' versions, and others lasting up to a minute longer. These two sets revealed him as an accomplished, grittily persuasive stylist, capable of stamping cover versions with his own individuality, and a convincing writer of anguished love songs in his own right.

Delroy had already enjoyed a monster hit with the Tams' "Dancing Mood", though the financial reward was apparently slim. The opening track of *Original Twelve*, Mac Davis' **Riding For A Fall**, was also first recorded by the Atlanta soul group, in 1964. The lyric – a warning to a former lover – suited Delroy's delivery perfectly, and it was another huge Jamaican hit. Other successes include the superb cover of the Temptations' **Get Ready**, its rhythm poised on the cusp of ska and rock steady, and the cover of Little Milton's **Gonna Make It**; Jamaican soul of the first rank. On other songs here – **Ungrateful Baby, Someone's Gonna Cry** – Delroy maintains the persona of a man emotionally wounded by love, but determined to carry on, as on **Troubled Man** and the rock steady masterpiece **True Believer In Love**. His declaration that he was "A true believer in love, and nothing's gonna change me now" – was nothing less than his personal manifesto. On the extended tracks like **Run Run** and **Conquer Me**, he delivered defiant, assertive lyrics with restraint but no diminution of power.

His transparent sincerity in all his performances only served further to endear him to his many fans; his expressive style, particularly his phrasing and timing, like those of Alton Ellis, became a strong influence on succeeding generations of artists, including such stars as Dennis Brown and Beres Hammond. Unlike his contemporaries John Holt and Ken Boothe, Delroy never enjoyed mainstream recognition in the 1970s. Nonetheless, he continued making excellent records, scoring massive Jamaican hits with producer Bunny Lee in the early 1970s ("Cool Operator", "Better Must Come"), and recording for the likes of Niney, Joe Gibbs, George 'Phil' Pratt and Gussie Clarke. His album *Sarge* was a commercial and artistic success mid-decade for producer Lloyd Charmers, particularly in the UK market.

Delroy Wilson continued recording and performing into the 1990s, but he died in late 1996 of a brain haemorrhage that resulted from the cirrhosis and subsequent liver failure brought on by his habitual use of white rum. His funeral – one of the largest ever accorded an artist – was attended by friends from the reggae business and politicians alike, including the Prime Minister. In the opinion of many, not least his longtime friend the producer Bunny Lee, he may well have been the greatest of the select band of Jamaican soul masters.

⮑ We almost chose **The Prime Of ...**, MCI, UK, 1997

92

Delroy Wilson

Sarge

LTD, 1976, JA; Charmers, 1998, UK

Recorded 1976. Delroy Wilson (vocals), Harold Butler (kbds), Val Douglas (bass), Willie Lindo (gtr), Michael Richard (drms), Roots Casanovas (brass), Derrick Stewart (drums), the Charmers (backing vocals). Produced by Lloyd Charmers.

By the mid-1970s – or so it was often perceived outside Jamaica – the entire focus of Jamaican music seemed to have swung over to Rastafarian-inspired cultural and spiritual themes. However, despite the number of performers hurriedly growing dreadlocks, and the way red, gold and green became the de rigueur colours for reggae album sleeves, the best-selling reggae single of 1976 – and not just in Jamaica, but all over the world – was Delroy Wilson's **I'm Still Waiting**.

A yearning love song written by Bob Marley, it had originally been recorded by the Wailers in the mid-'60s, in the Impressions-influenced doo-wop style they then favoured for ballads. Where the Wailers took it at a tortuously slow pace, Delroy's producer Lloyd 'Charmers' Tyrell slightly speeded things up, and gave it a much fuller and more contemporary arrangement. Similarly, Delroy's full-voiced vocal attack contrasted with Marley's gentle easing of the lyric. Naturally, an album followed, **Sarge**, on which all the tracks stuck to a similar format – one of Jamaican music's greatest vocal stylists singing an established Jamaican favourite, with the maximum of expression, over crisp, ultra-smooth Charmers-produced rhythms.

A gifted keyboard player and former member of the Uniques vocal group, Charmers had launched his first label at the start of the '70s. He successfully recorded vocals – including Ken Boothe's UK chart-topping "Everything I Own" – and sophisticated but popular instrumentals, such as "Breezing" from guitarist Willie Lindo.

Charmers' arrangements – and they were very much that – stamped class upon anything he recorded, and his approach was ideally suited to the veteran Wilson, whose vocal prowess and sheer sense of style had developed considerably from the spirited ska hits he'd cut as a child star at Studio One. He'd since been responsible for a series of rock steady gems recorded at Brentford Road, and applied his mature voice to emotive love songs throughout the first half of the '70s, scoring hits for Joe Gibbs, Bunny Lee, Sonia Pottinger, Gussie Clarke, Niney, Joseph Hookim and Jack Ruby. When called to, he was also capable of applying his warm tones to a cultural lyric but he never sounded more at home than when interpreting a quality soul hit.

Anyone who harbours doubts about reggae's reliance on the version (as opposed to the ceaseless pursuit of originality) should listen to Delroy Wilson's most accomplished post-Studio One album, which also happens to have sold by the cartload ever since its first appearance. There might not be one original song here, but there's enough of the singer's incomparable vocal style, as well as Lloyd Charmers' under-valued production skills, to make even the much-versioned My Conversation seem fresh. Some of the material might seem unlikely – Jerry Lee Lewis's country weepie Green Green Grass Of Home, Paul Simon's My Cecilia, Tom Paxton's Too Late For the Learning – but the approach works beautifully (someone obviously knew a good song when he heard it). Singing songs that were primarily associated in Jamaica with his main rivals – Slim Smith for "My Conversation" and Everybody Needs Love, Alton Ellis for Ain't That Loving You and Girl I've Got A Date, and Ken Boothe for I Don't Want To See You Cry – Delroy obviously faced the toughest comparisons, but he delivered something different every time.

➲ We almost chose **24 Super Hits**, Sonic Sounds, JA, 1992

93

Yabby You

Jesus Dread

Blood & Fire, 1997, UK

Recorded 1972–77. Produced by Vivian 'Yabby You' Jackson. Musicians include: Wayne Wade (vocals), Big Youth (deejay), Tappa Zukie (deejay), Trinity (deejay), Dillinger (deejay), Augustus Pablo (melodica, piano).

The singer-producer Yabby You (born Vivian Jackson, Kingston, 1946) occupies a unique place in the roots phase of reggae, not least because of his unusual take on Rastafarianism, which replaces Haile Selassie as the faith's central figure with Jesus Christ. Hence his **Jesus Dread** monicker, a title which has also been attached to this copious two-CD collection of his seminal 1970s work.

Jackson's career began in 1972, when he cut **Conquering Lion**, a record comparable in impact to the Abyssinians' "Satta Massagana" or Burning Spear's "Door Peeper". Its chanted chorus, "Yabby You", soon passed to Jackson himself, after would-be purchasers starting asking for "Yabby You". A little while later, the equally original **Love Thy Neighbour** appeared. Though initially pressed in small quantities – a mere one hundred copies, in the case of "Conquering Lion" – they made the enigmatic Jackson enough money to launch his Prophets label in 1974.

Most of the early releases on Prophets, including **Love Of Jah**, **Run Come Rally**, and **Warn the Nation**, are now regarded as roots classics. Except for **Jah Vengeance**, where the group's name became the Sons of Jah, they were credited to either Vivian Jackson and the Prophets, or just the Prophets. On the whole, Yabby sang lead vocals, but others among the Prophets' fluid membership sometimes stepped forward, as with Errol 'Dada' Smith's lead on "Warn the Nation". The singles were collected on a debut album known as *Conquering Lion* in Jamaica, and *Ram A Dam* in the UK. In the same period, Jackson also discovered the 13-year-old Wayne Wade, whose first record (not included here) was the sublime "Black Is Our Colour", a perfect blending of lovers and roots. Heavier roots outings from the sweet-voiced young singer followed. Often, as with Lord Of Lords, Wade's recut of "Conquering Lion", they expressed the same themes as their producer's own vocals.

In keeping with the trend of the times, Jackson issued compelling deejay versions of his most enduring rhythms. Alongside successful sides from such noted mikemen as Big Youth, Trinity, Dillinger, Tappa Zukie and Jah Stitch came a few instrumental cuts – saxophonist Tommy McCook and trombonist Don D Jnr's Fisherman Special, and McCook's Revenge and Death Trap are excellent examples. This set adds previously unreleased – and just as exemplary – sax versions of King Pharaoh's Plague and Chant Down Babylon Kingdom. Talking of 'versions', Jackson's association with King Tubby went back to when he voiced "Conquering Lion" at the Dub Master's studio, and he was among the first producers to have his 45s appear with dub sides mixed at Tubby's. The deconstructions of Yabby Youth and Run Come Rally are particularly outstanding.

If the fire-and-thunder imagery of his vision became tired in lesser hands, Jackson's palpable sincerity still makes these groundbreaking sides sound genuinely inspired and inspiring. *Jesus Dread* includes a phenomenal 47 tracks, featuring numerous additional versions of the classics on the original *Conquering Lion/Ram A Dam* album, plus the pick of the subsequent *Walls Of Jerusalem* and *Deliver Me From my Enemies* albums, and further singles. It stands not only as the definitive Yabby You selection, but as a cornerstone for any decent roots collection.

⊃ Almost chose **Michael Prophet: Serious Reasoning**, Island, UK, 1980

94

Yabby You

King Tubby's Prophesy Of Dub

Prophets, UK, 1976; Blood & Fire, UK, 1995

Recorded 1972–75. Engineered by King Tubby. Produced by Vivian 'Yabby You' Jackson.

The vinyl original of **King Tubby's Prophesy Of Dub** was released in 1976, in a limited UK press of five hundred copies and without a proper sleeve. Yabby You was by then established as one of Jamaica's leading singer-producers, concerned almost exclusively with what was known at the time as 'truth and rights' – the iniquities that had been dealt to the black race, and the coming dispensation.

From his debut single, "Conquering Lion", Yabby You had ensured complete control over his very individual work by producing it himself, and releasing the results on his own Prophets label. In addition to issuing tunes under the name of his own Prophets vocal group, he had also been taking similarly committed vocalists into the studio, including Dicky Burton, the very youthful Wayne Wade and Errol Alphonso, along with deejays like Big Youth, Trinity, Jah Stitch and Dillinger. As Yabby's relationship with King Tubby went back to 1972, when the most important figure in the development of dub was instrumental in the release of his first record, it's not surprising that all the singles on Prophets had their 'version' sides mixed by the Dub Master himself at his tiny Dromilly Avenue studio.

When the inevitable album's worth of dub cuts appeared, it easily met the expectations created by the epochal 45s. The first set on which Tubby took apart and reassembled Yabby's rhythms tackled most of his early classics to make them sound far rawer, while still managing to retain their very musical qualities. Most of the original vocals had been collected on the classic *Conquering Lion* album. Not unexpectedly, the title track's thunderous rhythm crops up here – as Conquering Dub – alongside equally impressive versions of "Run Come Rally", "Love Thy Neighbour" and "Jah Vengeance", and Errol Alphonso's stunning record of the previous year, "Chant Jah Victory". Another outstanding example of King Tubby's art was his treatment of the early Michael Rose gem, "Born Free", Rock Vibration, on which the flying cymbals of drummer Carlton 'Santa' Davis became virtually the lead instrument.

To the 1976 vinyl album's original twelve tracks, this beautifully packaged CD adds the dub sides of two much-sought-after instrumentals: Tommy McCook's "Revenge" – itself a cut of its producer's "Jah Vengeance" – and "Death Trap".

As with all the best dub, what is left out is as important as what's still there: great cavernous spaces yawn between the different instruments, throwing into sharp relief both the heavyweight bass lines shared between Aston 'Family Man' Barrett, Robbie Shakespeare, and Gladiator Clinton Fearon, and the way they're off-set by the drums of Carlton 'Santa' Davis, Studio One regular Leroy 'Horsemouth' Wallace, and Benbow Greary. Sometimes the horns of Tommy McCook, Bobby Ellis and Vincent Gordon hover at the edges of the music, just threatening to burst in, only to sound all the more uplifting when they actually appear in a sudden great flurry. (For more of the excellent horns work associated with Yabby's productions, check Tommy McCook and Bobby Ellis's *Blazing Horns* album, and *Beware Dub*, both released by the UK-based Grove Music a couple of years later.) The results that emerged when Yabby You's rhythms were taken through their paces on King Tubby's four-track mixing board have appeared on several albums, but this is the definitive expression of both producer's and engineer's powers.

➲ We almost chose **Meets Tommy McCook...**, Peacemaker, Canada, 1996

95

Various Artists

A Dee Jay Explosion Vol 1& 2

Heartbeat, 1992, US/UK

Recorded 1982. Deejays include Eek-A-Mouse, Welton Irie, Brigadier Jerry, Ranking Toyan, Lee Van Cleef, Nigger Kojak, Yellowman, Michigan & Smiley, Sister Nancy, Sassafrass, Johnny Ringo, Trinity. Produced by Mike Cacia.

The deejay is a crucial participant in Jamaican dancehall culture, but not until the dawn of the 1980s did reggae start to be called 'dancehall' music. Perhaps this was a reaction to the phenomenon of 'international' reggae, which by this time had settled on a handful of acts to represent the music to the world beyond Jamaica. On the island itself, everything revolved around the dancehalls, where sound systems tested new tunes and played dub cuts of old classics, over which deejays and singers delivered a constant flow of customized lyrics. Where international reggae had to conform to the formats and marketing cycles of major corporations, dancehall was much more in tune with its audience. A deejay could test out lyrics at a Saturday night dance, record on Sunday, and cut the record Monday. By mid-week it could be in every shop on the island.

The live recordings on **A Dee Jay Explosion**, on which a dozen deejays battle it out on the mike, portray the first stage of this local process with a powerful sense of off-the-cuff excitement. The authenticity of the atmosphere is helped immeasurably by the scratchy dubplates selected by Archie of Gemini Sound System, and the artists' banter and greetings to friends and 'supas' in the crowd. Heartbeat recorded two sessions at the famous Skateland Roller Disco at Half Way Tree in central

Kingston; three tracks by Michigan and Smiley, recorded at another dance in Spanish Town, fit in perfectly with the rest.

As well as a compendium of then-contemporary styles, this CD exemplifies the Jamaican deejay tradition, dating from 1950 and Count Machuki, the progenitor of modern rap. Deejay blossomed after U-Roy burst on the scene with King Tubby's Hi-Fi at the end of the 1960s; his influence continued throughout the 1970s, with followers like U-Brown and Ranking Joe. By the time this disc was recorded, Charlie Chaplin, Josey Wales, and Brigadier Jerry were upholding U-Roy's style in the dance; three good tracks from the under-recorded Brigadier show why his peers held him in such high esteem. Trinity and Ranking Toyan, also featured here, were perpetuating the 1970s' other main deejay style, as started by Big Youth on Lord Tipatone Hi-Fi. Rasta culture and rudeboy gunplay have long co-existed in both the ghetto and the dancehall; inevitably some deejays got caught up in the violence. Lee Van Cleef, Ranking Toyan, and Fat Head (heard here with Yellowman) all fell victim to Kingston's gun culture, in another parallel with 'gangsta' rap.

The rhythms heard here are the staples of dancehall; they have moved the crowd for three decades and continue to work to this day. As well as several original Studio One cuts, we also hear Gussie Clarke's version of "Full Up", a recut of a classic Studio One rhythm, used successfully for the Mighty Diamonds monster hit "Pass The Kouchie" in 1981. The lyrics Brigadier Jerry uses on his cut here (This One's Dedicated To You) were first used in dances by U-Brown; on You Don't Know Me As No Rum Drinker, Trinity adapts lyrics originally chatted by Ranking Joe on champion 1980s' sound Ray Symbolic Hi-Fi. This 'borrowing' is all part of the process; other lyrics were adapted from pop songs, Jamaican folk, nursery rhyme and street slang, to comment on and celebrate the milieu of the dancehall and its manners and mores – in other words, to 'nice up the dance'. This is the authentic Jamaican dancehall experience, in all its creativity and accessibility, a true people's medium.

⊃ We almost chose **King Stur-Gav Live ...**, Tamoki Wambesi, UK, 1997

96

Various Artists

Hardcore Ragga: The Music Works Dancehall Hits

Greensleeves, 1990, UK

Recorded 1988–90. Produced by Augustus 'Gussie' Clark. Artists include Gregory Isaacs, J.C. Lodge, Lady G, Shabba Ranks, Deborahe Glasgow, Home T, Cocoa Tea, Tiger, Krystal, Rebel Princess, Papa San.

Three years after the first digital hit from King Jammy, dancehall music took its next step forward. Once again, it was heralded by one ground-breaking single, from a producer whose career went back to the 1970s. **Augustus 'Gussie' Clarke** had started pro-ducing in his teens, making his initial impact with the deejays U-Roy, Big Youth and I-Roy. He always had an eye for the international market, and should have enjoyed crossover success in 1981 with the Mighty Diamonds' "Pass the Kouchie"; in the event, a bowdlerized version by UK pop-reggae group Musical Youth cleaned up outside Jamaica.

By 1987, Gussie was in control of his own studio, Music Works, which he intended to be Jamaica's answer to Motown – a completely professional organization, with in-house writers, that was to record only original rhythms. Things didn't work out quite as he hoped, but for a couple of years Gussie was responsi-ble for some highly innovative records, employing a high-tech sound that demonstrated how the new technology remained compatible with the musical values of late 1970s roots music.

The tune that launched Gussie's glossy new sound, Gregory Isaacs' **Rumours**, also brought the singer back after a couple of difficult years. Though not quite what it had been, his voice was entirely suited to the paranoid lyric about rumour mongers – and the Steely and Clevie rhythm was unbeatable.

Hardcore Ragga collects Gussie's most successful digital tunes. Starting with the Isaacs hit, it segues into J.C. Lodge's cut, Telephone Love, and the demand for Nuff Respect from the one female deejay then striking a chord with dancehall audiences, Lady G. As with any killer rhythm, the subsequent variations on the theme simply add to its power. Gregory's Mind Yu Dis follows, his paranoid perspective this time turned on those rudeboys foolish enough to disrespect him. As he says, "What you're picking up / I put down already." Shabba Ranks then rides the same rhythm, appositely adapting the lyric to the kind of serious soundclash business that has always been his forte.

The late UK lovers-rock singer Deborahe Glasgow also benefited from the Music Works touch, and her assertive Champion Lover is presented with Shabba's boastful Mr Lover Man answer disc. A further UK connection comes with the first track on another outstanding rhythm, Pirate's Anthem, where Shabba, with sweeter-sounding crooners Home T and Cocoa Tea, defends the illegal radio stations that were allowing people in England to hear new reggae. One of Gussie's major ploys towards broadening the popularity of dancehall took the form of placing women singers such as J.C. Lodge, Deborahe Glasgow, Krystal and Princess Rebel in 'combination' with roughhouse deejays like Shabba. Several fine examples are included here, but even more devastating is Papa San and Lady G's Round Table Talk, continuing the amusing marital discord heard on the two deejays' "Legal Rights" for Winston Riley. Lady G perhaps has the last word in this particular tiff, but Papa S comes into his own on Dancehall Good To We, which incorporates elements from an ancient mento song, and links modern performers to foundation deejays like King Stitt, U-Roy and Dennis Alcapone in an inspired tongue-twisting defence of dancehall music.

Unfortunately Gussie, who always had a glossy take on dancehall, was soon to move too far away from the music's life-blood.

⮑ Almost **Home-T, Shabba, Cocoa Tea: Holding On**, Greensleeves, 1988

97

Various Artists

Lovers Rock: Serious Selection Volume 1

Rewind Selecta, 1995, UK

Recorded 1975–80. Artists include Ruddy Thomas, Fil Callender, Jah Stitch, Horace Andy, Tappa Zukie, Matumbi, Barry Biggs, Portia Morgan, Louisa Marks, Bunny Maloney, Motions, Errol Dunkley, the Tamlins, Jean Adebambo.

Perhaps in part because it has been the one area of the music to give voice to the concerns of women, lovers rock has long been the most misunderstood facet of reggae. When the style emerged in the mid-1970s, it also faced the usual struggle experienced by any UK reggae in being accepted as the equal of music from Jamaica, and it has to be admitted that many of the early tunes displayed decidedly unsteady vocal techniques, often from girl singers who sounded as they were still worrying about their school reports. Nevertheless, tunes on labels like Lovers Rock itself – which gave the genre its name – Rite Sound, and Santic found a ready audience among working-class teenage girls in the British inner cities. This was a constituency who couldn't always identify with the diet of militant 'steppers' tunes offered by many of the sound systems of the time. Even in those formative years, the genre produced some classics, and it continued to develop throughout the next two decades.

In common with most of reggae, the main artery of lovers rock has always been the single, particularly the 12-inch variety, the rise of which coincided with that of the genre. Fortunately, a large number of excellent compilations have assembled the biggest hits; the *Pure Lovers* and *Lovers For Lovers* series are particularly reliable. For the newcomer, however, **Lovers Rock:**

Serious Selection Volume 1, the first in a three-part series compiled by radio DJ David Rodigan, makes the ideal introduction. To start with, it covers both the original UK variety, and the tunes that were cut in Jamaica as a response to their success in the British reggae charts. All but one of the thirteen tracks are also presented in their original 12-inch mixes, so they're guaranteed to bring back memories of the blues parties that were this music's natural habitat.

The disc that kickstarted things in 1975, the 14-year-old Louisa Marks' plaintive reading of Robert Parker's soul hit Caught You In a Lie, demonstrates that lack of maturity has never been as important as sincerity. Being produced by the top London sound system man of the time, Lloyd Coxsone, did no harm, either – nor did a rhythm from Dennis Bovell's superb band, Matumbi. Their own best remembered lovers hit, After Tonight, also makes an appearance.

Never fashionable with music journalists, lovers rock tunes have always relied on connecting with their audience in the most direct way – heard over a sound system at a dance. That means that a newcomer has always stood a good chance of having the latest boom tune. One classic example here is Let Me Be Your Angel from Portia Morgan, a record from an unknown that has achieved classic status. A more sophisticated take on lovers rock is Jean Adebambo's beautiful Paradise, a record that topped the UK reggae chart for several weeks, and served to signal the maturity of the genre.

The examples of Jamaican 'Yard style' lovers included here are just as strong. Horace Andy's Natty Dread A Weh She Want (complete with a toast from producer Tappa Zukie) appealed to both roots and lovers followers when it arrived as a Stars 12-inch in 1978. Ruddy Thomas' Key To The World and the Tamlins' rendition of Ting A Ling compete for consideration as the most soulful of the offerings from Jamaican singers, while Barry Biggs' Wide Awake In A Dream and Fil Callender's Baby My Love vie as the the most gloriously romantic.

➲ We almost chose **Lovers Rock Vol. 2**, Rewind Selecta, UK, 1995

98

Various Artists

Mojo Rock Steady

Heartbeat, 1994, US

Recorded 1966–73. Produced by Coxsone Dodd. Artists include Prince Francis, The Gaylads, Roland Alphonso, Denise Darlington, The Bassies, The Soul Brothers, The Minstrels, King Stitt, Alton Ellis and the Soul Vendors, The Clarendonians.

While Duke Reid might have pushed Clement 'Sir Coxsone' Dodd – temporarily – into second place during the rock steady era, there's no denying the enduring appeal of the rhythms that were built at Brentford Road in the late 1960s. As Reid moved further from the music's beginnings, substituting the refinements of Detroit and Chicago soul for the hard-edged rhythm and blues from which ska had grown, Sir Coxsone's rock steady retained a roughness that both glanced back at ska and anticipated the future. And if the Duke's Treasure Isle sound epitomized the romantic feel of rock steady, it has still been the Studio One rhythms that have been the most 'versioned' ever since. Several worthwhile compilations were released at the time, but the best collection of Studio One rock steady has to be the **Mojo Rock Steady** set – despite its rather odd history (and the inclusion of a couple of tracks that aren't actually rock steady!).

To cover its genesis first (take a deep breath): a twelve-track vinyl album called *Mojo Rock Steady* was released in Jamaica, by one of Coxsone Dodd's sons, in 1992. This not only had completely different packaging from the present CD, but one track that was not to reappear in either of its further incarnations. The sound quality made it obvious that the tracks had been dubbed from disc rather than master tapes, and because Dodd had not given permission for its release, it was quickly withdrawn. Ironically, even if it didn't include the title track (!), it was the best Studio One compilation to appear for years. An official vinyl variation was released the next year. Four of its thirteen tracks were different from the Coxsone Jnr issue, including the welcome addition of both the instrumental and deejay versions of Mojo Rock Steady. By Studio One standards none of that was too confusing, but then in 1994 Heartbeat, the US company with the largest Studio One reissue programme, stepped into the picture, releasing the present CD, which is essentially a compilation of the two vinyl albums, with a more generous sixteen tracks – including three which hadn't appeared on either of the vinyl issues. This was also the best in terms of sound quality.

Among the tracks that make at least one variation of the set essential for even long-term Studio One collectors is Alton Ellis and the Soul Vendors' Whipping the Prince, the very rare first cut of the perennial rhythm best known as "Death In the Arena". This original cut, a wicked Soul Vendors instrumental with occasional interjections from Alton Ellis, remains one of the most deadly 'sound burial' tunes ever – aimed straight at Prince Buster's head. The still under-acclaimed Gaylads triumph with two numbers – I'm Free, on which the trio declare they're at liberty from some no-longer-desired romantic entanglement, and the even more impressive Africa, a beautiful repatriation plea that was way ahead of its time, and revived by Dennis Brown in the next decade with only minimal change in the arrangement. Both the Bassies' beautiful gospel adaptation River Jordan, originally the flip of the Soul Vendors "Swing Easy", and the more obscure Minstrels' fine version of the Impressions' People Get Ready work as haunting cries for freedom. But perhaps the quality that lifts the selection far above the usual hit-and-miss Brentford Road compilation is the balance between quality vocals and instrumentals – with the saxophone of the late Roland Alphonso displayed to particularly good advantage.

➲ We almost chose **Showcase Vol. 1**, Heartbeat, US/UK, 1999

99

Various Artists

Rebel Music: An Anthology Of Reggae Music

Trojan, 1979, UK

Recorded 1970–75. Artists include Bob Andy, Derrick Harriott, Freddy McKay, Keith Hudson, U-Roy, Peter Tosh, the Heptones, Big Youth, Little Roy, Glen Brown, Junior Byles, Dennis Brown, Horace Andy, Gregory Isaacs, I-Roy, Michael Dyke.

The 'roots' explosion of the second half of the 1970s was clearly anticipated by the so-called **Rebel Music** of the decade's early years. Black consciousness and 'cultural' themes grew in popularity between 1968, when romantic rock steady gave way to rougher sounds, and 1975, when the waving of dreadlocks was expected at all reggae performances.

Yet the term 'rebel music' never principally referred to social or political rebellion; rather, it expressed the struggle of newer, smaller producers against the established order on the Kingston recording scene, as represented by Clement Dodd and Duke Reid. It just so happened that this new generation of producers, often from the same backgrounds as the performers, were more likely to sympathize with young ghetto singers and deejays, and felt a far greater need to experiment with every aspect of record production in order to make their mark. The period covered by this thoughtful two-CD compilation was perhaps the most adventurous in the entire history of Jamaican music, with a sense of the radical in what performers were saying entirely compatible with the latest innovations in studio technique.

Not that all the producers represented here were newcomers. Derrick Harriott's career in music, for example, went back to singing with the Jiving Juniors in the late 1950s, and he had owned his own label since 1962, while Lee Perry sang at Studio One in the ska era, and supervised sessions for Joe Gibbs before launching his own Upsetter imprint. Bunny Lee had already made his name producing rock steady and early reggae hits from such artists as the Uniques, Derrick Morgan and Pat Kelly. Even the old guard, in the form of both Clement Dodd and Duke Reid themselves, are represented here. But regardless of age or how established they may have been, it is indisputable that the approach of every producer here was informed by the onrush of fresh producers and performers into the Kingston studio scene.

Among the trailblazing producers included are Keith Hudson, Lee Perry, and Glen Brown. For something truly left-field, check Glen Brown's melodica instrumental 2 Wedden Skank, involving snatches of the "Wedding March", or Keith Hudson's eerie Melody Maker. The genius of Perry isn't demonstrated by one of his more eccentric pieces, but by Junior Byles expressing the apocalyptic vision of Beat Down Babylon over the kind of rhythm with which his producer's name was synonymous.

Further social and spiritual comment is found on Leroy Smart's God Helps the Man, Lloyd Parks' Slaving, and Dennis Brown's Concentration. Each sounds as if born of intensely felt experience, as do Michael Dyke's one record of note, Saturday Night Special, Peter Tosh's angry Them A Fe Get A Beatin' and the Heptones' Hypocrites. To show that innovative rhythms could support love songs just as well, try K.C. White's Anywhere But Nowhere or Horace Andy's You Are My Angel. Another important facet is represented by the deejays, whose tunes often combine a verbal street reality with an appropriate radical mix, as also true for at least one singing track: Horace Andy and Earl Flute's menacing Satan Side.

Sadly, there are no liner notes to put everything in context – and it does come with the same naff artwork as the 1979 vinyl press – but 28 innovative, daring, quirky, heartfelt and committed tracks make Rebel Music the most comprehensive introduction to the era currently available. Crucial music.

➲ We almost chose **Various: Observation Station**, Heartbeat, US/UK, 1990

100

Various Artists

Tougher Than Tough: The Story of Jamaican Music

Mango, 1993, UK/US

Recorded 1958–93. Artists include Derrick Morgan, the Wailers, Justin Hinds and the Dominoes, the Skatalites, Prince Buster, Desmond Dekker, U-Roy, Big Youth, Dennis Brown, the Upsetters, Burning Spear, Max Romeo, Culture, Gregory Isaacs, Frankie Paul, Barrington Levy, Tenor Saw, Shabba Ranks, Buju Banton, Shaggy.

Given the importance of 'various artists' compilations in the reggae marketplace, it might seem surprising that there have been so few attempts to tell the history of the music in this way. While the *Trojan Story* triple set did a worthwhile job for the period up to its release in 1971, anyone interested in an informed aural overview of the development of reggae had to wait over two decades before Island released the four-CD **Tougher than Tough** set (compiled by one of the authors of this volume). Book-ended by the Folkes Brothers' original cut of Oh Carolina, from the late 1950s, and Shaggy's ragga updating of the tune from 1993, it presents the most comprehensive story to date of Jamaican music, as told through 95 of the island's major hits.

The shuffles of the late '50s, with which the first disc begins, were essentially Jamaican attempts to emulate US r'n'b, but Theophilus Beckford's Easy Snappin', from 1959, already shows Jamaican music taking on a distinctive character. Such records led to the first musical style to be associated with the island. Driving instrumental ska is represented by records like Don Drummond's Man In the Street, while the often under-valued vocal variety has its place with classics from, among others, Prince Buster, Derrick Morgan and Justin Hinds. The shift on from ska could not be better illustrated than by Delroy Wilson's bittersweet Dancing Mood, while the enduring appeal of fully developed rock steady is embodied in the Techniques' Queen Majesty and the Jamaicans' Ba Ba Boom.

The second disc charts the different styles that went under the name of reggae itself between 1968 and 1974, including the fast rhythms that entered the UK pop charts, and the establishment of two crucial facets – toasting over vocal hits by deejays like U-Roy, and social commentaries from a Rastafarian perspective. The full flowering of the 'roots' phase of the 1970s is covered in the next disc, with such names as the Mighty Diamonds, Burning Spear, and Jacob Miller, but there's still space for Delroy Wilson's sublime interpretation of I'm Still Waiting, and the Wailing Souls' Bredda Gravalicious.

The final disc explores the period after Marley's death, when many outside commentators lost the plot completely. A revelation to some listeners will be hearing the excitement and inventiveness of quintessential dancehall hits such as Wayne Smith's ground-breaking Under Me Sleng Teng, Half Pint's Greetings, Supercat's Boops, and Pinchers' Bandolero.

The sheer number of major records here makes *Tougher Than Tough* an ideal introduction for the newcomer. But like any worthwhile compilation, it enables even long-term followers to hear the familiar with fresh ears. The selection is unashamedly populist, and 'pop reggae' favourites – from Millie's My Boy Lollipop to Althea and Donna's Up Town Top Ranking – are placed in their rightful context as major hits in Jamaica. Even more important, this set gives the many people who only know the crossover successes a chance to hear some of the tunes that were just as popular in the reggae world. And it comes complete with a lavish 65-page booklet, to put everything in context.

> ⮞ There's really no choice on this one